Lewis WAY – A BIOGRAPHY

By Geoffrey Henderson

Published by HTS Media
Copyright © 2014 by Geoffrey Henderson
All rights reserved
ISBN 978-0-9555304-1-8
Printed in Great Britain by 4edge Limited

Also by Geoffrey Henderson
All Love – A Biography of Ridley Herschell

Front cover picture: 'View of Stansted Park' watercolour 18th century,
English school
Courtesy of The Trustees of Stansted Park Foundation

For further information contact Geoffrey Henderson at
info@htsmedia.com

Dedication

To Stuart Cohen who introduced me to Lewis Way

FOREWORD
By Kelvin Crombie

Some readers of books prefer novels; some prefer historical-novels; while others prefer the very pragmatic history only versions with not one iota of fiction. Within this latter category there are those for whom the more footnotes the better, so they can indulge in as much information as possible, while others prefer fewer footnotes (notes at the end of each chapter or at the end of the book being more preferable) so the flow in the narrative is not unnecessarily interrupted by what they might call 'trivia.'

Geoffrey Henderson's Lewis Way - A Biography, is by no means a novel, but the storyline is such that it could almost have been written by a novelist. It is full of plots and intrigues, rises and falls, that it could quite easily be turned into one of the classic BBC 19th century series.

It is also not an historical-novel, but one could almost imagine a Leon Uris or a James A Michener getting hold of this story and turning into a world famous best-seller akin to Exodus or The Source.

In the final analysis, though, it is a history book, but a history book of the second of those above stated history book categories – with not too many footnotes so as to stop the flow of the narrative. The balance, I found, is just about right.

Just about right for what! Although I happen to be one of those who prefer either a historical novel, or a history book with all the footnotes the author can provide (and at the bottom of the page thank you very much), I sense that Geoffrey's book 'is just about right' for fitting all three categories: it reads as a novel, it has enough history for it to actually be classified as an historical novel, yet it is in the final analysis, a real fair dinkum – history book.

What more could one ask for.

I had the great joy and privilege to serve with one of the principle characters of the book, the London Society (or CMJ) for quite a few years, and for much of that time I had the even greater privilege of researching and writing upon that Society's great history and heritage. With that having been said I should be somewhat qualified to speak about a subject matter, the life and ministry of Lewis Way, which is at the very core of the life of CMJ.

When I completed reading the proof copy sent to me, I instinctively inscribed (in pencil!) on the last page in big letters: 'BRAVO – Great Read.' Not only did I learn new things in Geoffrey's book, but additionally for the first time could see some connection points which had previously eluded me.

This book has brought one of the great, yet unheralded characters of British 19th century Evangelicalism and of Jewish-Christian relations - Lewis Way - into the open, in a way perhaps never hitherto done in other publications. Bravo Geoffrey, you have given to us what I believe is a jolly good read. May many others, be they Christian, Jewish, secular, novel readers or historians, have the opportunity of reading and enjoying and being so well instructed in some core matters, as I have been.

Chapter 1

There is a tide in the affairs of men.
Which, taken at the flood, leads on to fortune;
Omitted, all the voyage of their life
Is bound in shallows and in miseries.
On such a full sea are we now afloat,
And we must take the current when it serves,
Or lose our ventures.

William Shakespeare, *Julius Caesar*

John Way, Chief Clerk to the King's Bench Division of His Majesty's High Court of Justice walked briskly through London's Temple Garden with his solicitor, Andrew Edge, at his side.

Autumn leaves fell gently and a cool wind drifting across the garden from the Thames brought chill memories of the icy spring of 1799. John clutched momentarily at his snuff-coloured brown suit jacket and checked the buttons on his canary yellow waistcoat. At sixty-eight he wasn't getting any younger and his health, never of the best, was failing steadily. He rested for a moment on his long gold-headed cane.

Sadly, the wind drifting from the River Thames carried more than the promise of spring. In John's younger days London's river had supported fishing on an industrial scale, catching and selling a whole range of species which included lobsters and even salmon. But by the start of the 19th century raw sewage entering the river was becoming the source of a less pleasant breeze and, by the second decade of the 1800s Londoners had begun to illegally connect their overflowing cesspits to surface water drains which directly entered the Thames, the capital's main source of drinking water. The scented handkerchief, carried by men and women, was sometimes more than a lover's token or a dandy's affectation.

The King whose "bench" John Way was Chief Clerk to was George III, 'Farmer George' to the people, King of Great Britain and King of Ireland, and the year was 1800. The two lawyers were heading for Paper Buildings, an elongated four storey brick edifice housing a large number of overworked legal professionals. It was originally built from timber, lath and plaster, a construction method commonly known as "paper work", hence the name, even though by the nineteenth century it was more firmly constructed in brick. It remains to this day in the grounds of the Inner Temple, one of the four London Inns of Court, home to the English and Welsh legal profession.

One of the occupants of Paper Buildings had the same surname as the Chief Clerk but was not related to him. Until then John Way was not even aware of Lewis Way's existence. But as they moved through the dimly lit corridors John was struck by the name above one of the dark oak doors, Lewis Way, number eleven. By tradition the title of King's Counsel, K.C., was not added to his name at the Inns of Court but John would have known these were all barristers' chambers.

Why such a minor coincidence should have meant so much to John Way will become clear in time but for now it is enough to say he thought it was important to make this man's acquaintance and, finding Lewis was on holiday in Devonshire, instructed his trusty solicitor, Mr Edge, to make contact at the earliest opportunity on his return.

Meanwhile there was work to be done, though not necessarily as Chief Clerk. That job rather took care of itself and the Chief Clerk was not expected to get very deeply involved with the day to day routine. That was dealt with, very efficiently, by a team of low paid underlings. John Way didn't really need to be there at all except that he also acted as confidential clerk and agent to the Earl of Mansfield, Lord Chief Justice of the King's Bench since 1756. And the Earl of Mansfield, formerly plain William Mansfield, had appointed John to the post, which was in his gift, in 1778.[1]

John Way had been in service with William Mansfield for over forty years and had proved himself a very good household manager having started his career as a liveried footman. The Earl himself had no children and, after Gabriel Way died in 1755, John had no father in his life from the age of twenty-three. And so an informal father-son relationship seems to have developed between the two men, William Mansfield being twenty-seven years older than John. The relationship was based on trust and John's natural ability as an administrator and, from time to time perhaps, a fixer.

---

[1] The vacancy had occurred on the death of the previous incumbents William Lee and John Antonie.

Little is known of John's early education. He was born in Bridport, Dorset in 1732 and attended the small village school. Lewis Way also had his roots in Bridport but they do not seem to have been related to each other, the name was common enough. John's mother, Ann Raymond, to whom he was very close, seems to have provided some further education for him, probably at home. He may have worked for his father, Gabriel, described as a merchant from Holebrook, Dorset, but when he died in 1755 John found himself in service with the Earl of Mansfield in order to support himself and his mother.

In religious observance John was a Methodist at a time when its links with the Church of England were under great strain following the death of its charismatic founder John Wesley in 1791.

Such was the relationship between John Way and Lord Mansfield that John was admitted to Lincoln's Inn on 5th November 1757 to train as a barrister, although he was never actually called to the bar. As his namesake Lewis Way would discover, there wasn't a fortune to be made as a barrister at that time. On the other hand certain court positions, in the gift of his Lordship, could be very lucrative indeed.

The father-son relationship between the two men however did not extend to John inheriting the family fortunes of the 1st Earl of Mansfield and the Earl's considerable wealth would eventually go to his nephew, David.[2] But, courtesy

---

[2] David Murray, 2nd Earl of Mansfield (1727-1796)

of his Lordship, John could enjoy the rewards of a number of senior Court positions including:

Chief Clerk on Pleas Side
Clerk of the Day Rules
Custodes Brevium
Clerk of the Errors[3]

In 1799 a House of Commons Select Committee had reported on court fees and their distribution and it reveals that the net receipts for the position of Chief Clerk[4] in 1797 were £5,396. This was the most lucrative post but John only held it in trust for the Earl of Mansfield's nephew David and his heirs. However, John was allowed to deduct the not insignificant sum of £1,200 per annum for himself.

It is very difficult to calculate a realistic modern equivalent of that income but the average income in England in 1800 was about £20 a year. A British Army Private in the Infantry would earn a shilling a day which was £18.25 a year. A Captain could earn £155.12 a year[5] and was expected to put himself in harm's way and risk his life for King and country for that. For the office of Chief Clerk the Earl of Mansfield did nothing, David Murray did nothing and John Way did nothing. And so, in the course of time, John, through prudent investment in property, would become a very wealthy man.

---

[3] Browne's General Law-List for the Year 1782
[4] Full title, Chief Clerk or Prothonotary of the Court of King's Bench
[5] Source: www.napoleonguide.com/ukwages.htm

In 1764 John Way married Mary Poole, the daughter of John Poole, a Kensington attorney of Salisbury Court, Fleet Street. Sadly that marriage was not blessed with children and therein lies the reason for John's interest in his namesake, Lewis Way.

Chapter 2

"There's money, and then there's class. The two are often separated."

Kate Jacobs, *The Friday Night Knitting Club*, 2007

When Lewis Way returned to his dull London chambers from the glittering whirl of the Exeter Ball, probably the foremost social event of the year in that part of Devon, he had only one thing on his mind - the niece of his eminent host, the beautiful Mary Drewe, youngest daughter of the Revd Herman Drewe, brother of the very wealthy Sir Thomas Drewe.

Mary was just twenty and described as "a creature of radiant and captivating beauty."[6] Lewis was twenty-eight, second son of bluff Squire Benjamin Way and a single man in want of a wife, but, unlike Jane Austen's Fitzwilliam Darcy, not yet in possession of a good fortune, or even a small one. He was, however, an intelligent, handsome and likeable young man with an assured career in the law and a good family. Dressed by his London tailor with high collar and cravat beneath a wise, handsome face he certainly cut a dash with the provincial ladies of Exeter. But would that be enough to attract Mary's family and her significant fortune?

---

[6] *The Ways of Yesterday*, A.M.W. Stirling, 1930

Lewis Way was a victim of, or at least a participant in, the inheritance system of *primogeniture,* an ancient custom which permitted the first-born son of a family to inherit all the family property and wealth, and indeed all its debts. Lewis was second-born to his brother Benjamin and so, as British television costume drama has shown us over the years the girls joined in the undignified struggle to find rich husbands and the younger boys were sent out to the Army, the Church or, as in Lewis's case, the Law to make a living. The French Revolution of 1789 had recently swept away the undemocratic burden of *primogeniture* throughout most of Europe but England would retain the source of family drama and dynastic strife for many years to come before it was abolished in 1925.

So Lewis had the class, but not the money. He had joined in the ritual search for a wife and offered his heart to the lovely Mary who, with her social connections, and her potential wealth might have aspired to a better match than that offered by this second-son from the Inns-of-Court. Her family, the Drewes of Grange could trace their line back to 1133, the days of Henry II (great-grandson of William the Conqueror no less) while Lewis could only see his way back five hundred years to the time of Edward II (1307). But that might just be enough if only he could raise some serious cash before Mary had somebody else's name at the top of her *programme du bal,* her very popular dance card.

Now, it may have been Providential or it may have been chance, but it just happens that the other Mr Way, John Way of Portugal Row, Lincoln's Inn Fields had just the opposite condition, no pedigree to speak of but rather a lot of money.

So, this John Way, in the autumn of his years and, finding himself without a suitable heir had, until he met Lewis Way, been seeking to establish a kind of retrospective dynasty by leaving his fortune to a distant relation, a "kinsman" of his mother, the Revd Gregory Syndercombe, Rector of Symondsbury near John's home town of Bridport. The Rector had apparently shown John some simple Christian kindness in the past and that led John to think his money would not be wasted in the Rector's altruistic hands. It seems that John Way had spent his life in a very brutal world of legal and moral corruption, protecting his master Lord Mansfield from the less pleasant effects of power in a world of slavery abroad and poverty at home. For this reason he sought a charitable home for his wealth and a little recognition for his family name in a class-ridden society. Reform was coming, revolution was in the air and Napoleon could invade at any time but Judaeo-Christian values remained the same and an Anglican clergyman like Gregory Syndercombe represented some kind of continuity in the changing world of Thomas Paine's Age of Reason.

The good Rector of Symondsbury, the aforementioned Gregory Syndercombe, had a daughter called Elizabeth Diana and she would receive a £20,000 legacy from John Way[7], a very significant sum, probably £700,000 today. The Rector would in turn receive £60,000 followed by the

---

[7] The same amount Jane Eyre would fictionally inherit in 1847 (*Jane Eyre*, Charlotte Brontë, chapter 33).

residue of John's estate which would be another £300,000 or so, ten to twenty million pounds of spending power today. The son, also Gregory, would, of course, inherit this on the death of his father.

John Way, in his desire to add some social credibility to his great wealth, often called 'new money', had added one small condition: the Syndercombe family must change its name to Raymond, John's mother's maiden name, before they could inherit. John's will stated clearly:

"......that the said Gregory Syndercombe and his heirs do and shall from my decease take and use the surname of Raymond only, in lieu of Syndercombe, after the surname of my family on the maternal side by which we are allied."

John wanted to form an alliance with the upmarket Syndercombes. They must become the family of the childless John Way and Gregory Syndercombe might then represent the son John never had. Such was the arrangement of John Way's will at the turn of the century and the Syndercombes would actually agree to it. John had made worse deals in his time. Gregory Syndercombe's son and heir would become Gregory Raymond under a document signed by the King himself at Whitehall on 11th September 1804.[8] Sadly for John Way, Gregory Raymond

---

[8] Whitehall, September 11, 1804: The King has been pleased to grant unto Gregory Syndercombe, jun. of Symondsbury, in the County of Dorset, Esq. His Royal Licence and Authority that he may take and use the Surname of Raymond only in lieu of that of Syndercombe, in Compliance with a Condition in the Will of his Kinsman John Way, late of Lincoln's-Inn-Fields, in the County of Middlesex, Esq; deceased.

would die childless in 1863 and the 'dynasty' he had tried to create just ground to a halt. The rest of the Syndercombe family still benefited from the input of cash and carried on as before, making other liaisons. Such was the brutality of the class system in the 19th century. But there would be a bitter twist in the tail for the Syndercombe family with the prospect of a new alliance for John with Lewis Way and his family, the Ways of Denham. John Way was about to arrange a life-changing meeting with the impoverished Lewis Way, King's Counsel of the Inner Temple.

And also to order, that His Majesty's concession and Declaration be recorded in His College of Arms.

Chapter 3

Labour was the first price, the original purchase-money that was paid for all things. It was not by gold or by silver, but by labour, that all the wealth of the world was originally purchased.

Adam Smith, *An Inquiry into the Nature and Causes of the Wealth of Nations,* 1776

Lewis Way was a kind man in an unkind world. He was one of those happy Christians who had no need for a dramatic Road to Damascus conversion. He had heard the Gospel at an early age, probably from his maternal grandmother[9], believed every word of it and acted on it, more or less. This, of course, did not make Lewis a great saint, as we shall discover, but, having the instinctive wisdom of Dostoyevsky's Prince Myshkin[10] coupled with a childlike trust in his fellow human beings he would leave the world a slightly better place than when he entered it.

Lewis was born to Benjamin and Elizabeth Ann on 11th February 1772 in the family's three storey London residence at Sackville Street, off Piccadilly. This was the less fashionable side of Piccadilly, as Oscar Wilde's Lady Bracknell might have said,[11] but still an address that made

---

[9] Catherine Cooke née Sleech (1720-1773).
[10] *The Idiot,* Fyodor Dostoyevsky.
[11] Oscar Wilde, *The Importance of Being Earnest,* 1895

a statement about his family, the Ways of Denham. The real family home of Denham Place in Buckinghamshire was, and still is, a superb late 17th century country house set in seemingly endless grounds and woods with multifaceted vistas across the Colne Valley and the Chiltern hills. It speaks of security, comfort and affluence in an age of revolution. Lewis's father, known as Squire Benjamin Way, was a Fellow of the Royal Society and, like his father before him was Sub-Governor of the South Sea Company[12] and President of Guy's Hospital as well as Governor of the Society for the Propagation of the Gospel in Foreign Parts. His great-grandfather, another Benjamin, is described simply as a slave trader[13], and therein lies a story and the foundation of the Way family's fortunes.

Lewis was the third of sixteen children, three of whom did not survive infancy. The six surviving girls led a very strict and sheltered life never being introduced into society, apart from an occasional trip to London. Only Mary Ann and Charlotte would marry and neither had children. Lewis's upbringing was strict in his stern father's house, surrounded as he often was by seemingly dour Evangelical clergymen, relieved only occasionally by visits to his uncle, Lord Sheffield at Sheffield Park in Sussex,[14] of whom he was very fond.

---

[12] A British multi-million pound trading company founded in 1711

[13] "In 1707 London slave trader Benjamin Way informed the Commission for Trade and Plantations that the only reason there was not a surplus of black labour was 'the Spanish being at hand to take off what can there be spared at a considerable Profit." *The Forgotten Trade*, Nigel Tattersfield, 1990, p. 352

[14] John Baker-Holroyd (1771-1863)

He was educated initially by his maternal grandmother Catherine,[15] and she would have him read to her from the popular sermons of the Revd Hugh Blair[16] whose first of five heavy volumes had been published in 1777. By the time the third of the five tomes was published Lewis had been packed off to Eton College, but no doubt would read to his grandmother in the holidays. His maternal grandfather had been headmaster of Eton College in 1772 so Lewis's place was secured from birth.

In spite of the clerical presence at Denham, or perhaps because of it, Lewis hoped to go into the Church as a career, but it was not to be. According to his father Lewis was "too clever" for the Church and, anyway, his brother William "the Bumble" had been set aside for the family living by his grandfather.[17] So, on graduating from Merton College, Oxford in 1796, Lewis would read for the Bar at Lincoln's Inn where, a few years later, he was to meet the man who would change his life forever.

The mysterious John Way entered the chambers of Lewis Way with a hint of the deference he had never quite lost, or perhaps he had retained it as a defence that ironic self-deprecation can bring in the face of unearned privilege. But Lewis disarmed him immediately with his natural charm and honesty, returning deference to John as his elder and a source of professional wisdom. It soon became clear, if unspoken, that there were mutual benefits to be had from this introduction as well as friendship.

---

[15] Catherine Sleech
[16] Hugh Blair (1718-1800)
[17] 1798: Rector of Denham and Vicar of Hedgerley, Bucks

Like the legal adversaries they might have been[18] the two men began to assess each other. The opening gambit of the mutual surname soon wore thin. The name was popular in Devon and they simply were not related. John would have already established that through his resourceful solicitor Mr Edge and Lewis's family tree had no known gaps in it. After a number of meetings John made the first serious move. One of the two MPs for Bridport the brave and flamboyant Charles Sturt[19] was likely to give up his parliamentary seat in the near future as his wife's colourful affair with the Marquis of Blandford, son of the Duke of Marlborough became public and his own long-standing *liaison* with Madame Krumpholtz followed close behind in the public domain.

John Way had given up the idea of becoming an MP for his hometown himself. Apparently given the opportunity he had declined on the grounds that "the pecuniary sacrifice would over-balance the gratification," a fancy way of saying he could make a lot more money in the day job. In fact MPs were not paid a salary at all at that time. Lewis, on the other hand, could still practice as a barrister and John would cover his expenses as an MP. All this, apparently, so that John could have some vicarious connection with the great and the good through his name. In addition to this offer, or as an alternative, John offered to arrange a marriage between Lewis and the daughter of the Revd Gregory Syndercombe who stood to gain £20,000 from John's will. At this stage Lewis had to confess that he

---

[18] The adversarial system would not actually be introduced for some years, promoted by Lewis Way's contemporary at Lincoln's Inn, William Garrow.

[19] Charles Sturt (1764-1812)

was carrying a flame for a lady in Devonshire, the lovely Mary Drewe, but did not have the means to ask for her hand in marriage. He could not accept the offer from John even if the Rector's daughter were willing.

This seems to have touched John in a way he had not experienced for a long time, if ever. Lewis was willing to turn down a wife with £20,000 and whatever John would add to that as a gift or dowry. John's own marriage to Mary Poole seems to have been a more mercenary affair. In his will, with reference to his wife, John writes:

"I do hereby ratify and confirm the settlement made upon her at our marriage though unfairly obtained from me by her father........."

He is clearly bitter about this un-named sum and although he leave's Mary comfortably off he never considers leaving her his main fortune.

At this point there is a change of heart in John. He offers Lewis a cheque for £1,000 in order that he might marry Mary Drewe. There would be no real benefit to John in that this would be a society wedding to which he probably would not be invited and would play no important role whereas he would have been a serious benefactor to the Rector, Gregory Syndercombe, who had already agreed to change their family name for money.

It seems that John had been moved by Lewis's simple love and may well have learned something of his sincere Christian faith in their time together. John in his turn may have introduced Lewis to the Revd Basil Woodd[20], preacher at the Bentinck Chapel, Marylebone which John attended. Basil Woodd, another beneficiary of John's will, would later become involved with Lewis in the work of the London Society for Promoting Christianity among the Jews, also known as the Jew's Society or simply the London Society as we will call it from now on. It was a small, cosy world they all inhabited, the last idyllic days before the Industrial Revolution overtook the world of the landed gentry. Napoleon never did invade England, but the mill and the steam engine soon would.

Lewis accepted the thousand pound cheque and the wedding was arranged for 31st December 1801. On 15th December 1801 John made a final change to his will:

"I John Way of Lincoln's Inn Fields Esquire do make this my fourth Codicil to my last Will bearing date 15th December 1801 and desire it may be added and taken as part thereof.
And first I revoke the devise and bequest in my said will to the Revd Gregory Syndercombe of the residue of my personal estate and effects and do hereby give and devise the said residue of my said personal estate and effects unto Lewis Way of Boswell Court Esquire to and for his own proper use and benefit and do appoint him a joint Executor of my will and codicils with the said Revd Dr Gregory Syndercombe and Edward Hilliard Esquire and I also give unto the said Lewis Way the sum of five thousand pounds Bank annuities specifically to and for his own use."

This "residue" would amount to £300,000 ($486,000), the equivalent today of at least ten million pounds. Having

---

[20] Basil Woodd (1760-1831)

lost out on the big money Gregory Syndercombe would have to make do with a total of £80,000 ($129,600) for the name change, and he did.

A direct comparison of these vast amounts of money in today's values is all but impossible. For example Lewis couldn't have bought a top-of-the-range Jaguar XF or a private Learjet, however rich he was. But he *could* have bought vast amounts of land and property which might have represented security for his family for generations to come, if he chose to keep them. The interest alone on Gregory Syndercombe's £80,000 would more than cover the lifestyle envisaged by Marianne Dashwood in Jane Austen's *Sense and Sensibility*, published in 1811:

"And yet two thousand-a-year is a very moderate income," said Marianne, "A family cannot well be maintained on a smaller. I am sure I am not extravagant in my demands. A proper establishment of servants, a carriage, perhaps two, and hunters, cannot be supported on less."

Today £300,000 would buy a fairly modest family house in parts of London but, as we shall see, Lewis would set his sights on something far more extravagant for just half that amount.

Lewis's life and that of many others was about to change in ways he could never have imagined. John Way died on 18th August 1804 and Lewis duly inherited. He honoured John Way in a manner he would have been very happy with. John was buried in a stone tomb in the Church of St Mary, Acton, close to his wife and mother. Lewis added a tall obelisk and put his own family coat of arms on it in stone. It is there to this day; proof that John had finally arrived, and joined the *other* Way family, at least in spirit.

Chapter 4

I've seen the smiling of Fortune beguiling,
I've felt all its favours and found its decay.

Alison Cockburn, *The Flowers of the Forest*

The Parish and Priory Church of St Mary, Totnes lies about twenty-two miles south of Exeter at the head of the River Dart in Devonshire. The town lies in the heart of what is justly designated today as an 'Area of Outstanding Natural Beauty,' seemingly endless vistas of moors, mountains and meadows with peaceful woods and wetlands stretching out as far as a horse-drawn *barouche* carriage could carry you.

The parish church was rebuilt on its original site between 1432 and 1460 and would be restored, rather clumsily some say, by Sir George Gilbert Scott much later in the nineteenth century to look the way it does today. And here, beneath its lofty arcades and red sandstone tower Lewis Way and Mary Drewe would be married on the very last day of 1801. Mary would have been dressed modestly, though probably not in white and without a veil as popularised by Queen Victoria. Fashionable colours during the Regency period included blue, pink, and green. From what we know of Mary she would not have dressed extravagantly and would have worn her wedding dress on other occasions in the future. She might have worn a hat with flowers in her hair and Lewis and his best man would certainly have worn top hats to go with their classic Georgian dark suits with three-quarter cutaway jackets, waistcoats and bright cravats. It would have been a small family affair following the 1662 Book of Common Prayer.

Not surprisingly Lewis's parents did not make the journey to Totnes. His father Benjamin was over sixty and in poor health. His mother, Elizabeth Ann, though younger, had borne sixteen children and would not undertake such a journey by mail coach. The railway today makes light work of the trip in three hours or less from London but in 1801 there was no Paddington station and the railway would not reach Totnes until 1847. In fact there would be no serious steam passenger railway service at all in England until the Stockton and Darlington Railway of 1825.

Tarmac roads were still a hundred years away but by the middle of the 19th century gleaming stagecoaches would be running between London and Exeter in as little as sixteen and a half hours. However, at the turn of the 18th century mail coaches were only making the trip in about twenty-four. Roads were still rough and even the well-defended, fast moving mail coaches were not immune to attack by highwaymen. Hounslow Heath and Bagshot Heath were favourite spots for highwaymen on the road to Exeter. So the groom's family, however well off, could not travel comfortably or even safely to glorious Devon on gravel roads in the cold winter of 1801/02.

After their short honeymoon in Wells, Bath and Durham Lewis took his new wife down to Denham to visit his parents. Mary was well received by the elder Mrs Way who calls her "the darling Lewis has so well described her to be."[21]

The couple had settled in London at 31 Spring Gardens, a substantial three storey town house off the Mall between Admiralty Arch and Trafalgar Square. The house was officially occupied from 1799 to 1803 by diplomat and fellow Old Etonian John Hookham Frere who seems to have lent it to them while he was working in Lisbon and Madrid. On his return in 1803 the couple moved back to Lewis's home at Boswell Court, closer to the Inner Temple and his freehold chambers there.

Six months after the wedding, on 6th June 1802, Lewis belatedly wrote to his namesake and friend, John Way. Addressing him respectfully as 'Dear Sir' Lewis makes rather vague suggestions as to how his now pregnant bride might meet the wife of his elderly benefactor:

"...if it would be agreeable to you and Mrs Way to take a drive after dinner tomorrow we should be happy to see you early at tea as we expect Mrs G. Way[22] and her family and they return in the evening to Ealing."

He adds, rather unhelpfully:

"....we should be very happy to wait upon you any other evening you will have the goodness to appoint."

---

[21] *The Ways of Yesterday*, A.M.W. Stirling, 1930
[22] Probably Ann Frances née Paxton, recent widow of Gregory Lewis Way

This is the man who invited Lewis to his home in rural Acton and gave him a cheque for £1,000 which probably clinched the marriage to his "darling." We can only assume time has muddied the waters of his friendship with John Way. Lewis clearly did not anticipate the fortune that was coming his way when John died just two years later. Although he may have harboured some expectations, as a cynical lawyer he would write:

"The singular attentions shown to me for years past by a perfect stranger, were too significant not to lead to certain conclusions, but the uncertainty of all testamentary matters kept my mind indifferent to these, and as to the extent of what my benefactor has done for me it never even entered into my dreams, as they were never those of avarice."

In February 1803 Lewis and Mary's first child, Lewis, was born. He already had a place at Eton and a very large inheritance. But it was not to be, and the younger Lewis, like so many children at that time, died within a year. All the money in the world would not have saved him and Lewis Way knew that very well.

Chapter 5

"Burn their synagogues and schools, what will not burn bury with earth, that neither stone nor rubbish remain. In like manner break into and destroy their homes. Take away their prayer books and Talmuds, in which there is nothing but Godlessness, lies, cursing and swearing."

Martin Luther, *The Jews and Their Lies*, 1543

It is not clear when Lewis Way began to take an interest in so-called apocalyptic writings, the Jewish prophetical works that grew out of their exile in Babylon, culminating, for Christians, in the Biblical book of Revelation or the Apocalypse. But his early life among Anglican Evangelical clergy and divines must have introduced him to the fashionable eschatological ideas about the end times and the return of the Jewish people to the Land of Israel. The dramatic and sometimes bloodthirsty visions of the Apocalypse were irresistible to this cruel age. Many Christians saw them as a reality for the near future, others as mostly allegorical but still important and meaningful. Jesus would certainly return but the circumstances, and sometimes even the time and place, were often the subject of heated discussion.

For nearly two thousand years the Jewish people had been exiled around the world after they were finally expelled from Israel by the Romans in AD 135. This had become known as the *Diaspora* or dispersion and followed from the destruction of the Jerusalem Temple in AD 70. For most of that time and in most places they were treated as outcasts in the world and their connection with the founding of Christianity through the Jewish Messiah Jesus was gradually more or less forgotten. Within four hundred years of the Crucifixion of Jesus his thousands of Jewish followers had been overtaken by 'pagan' believers who more or less rejected any role for the Jews in the on-going work of Jesus through his Church in the world. On 27th February 380, the Roman Emperor Theodosius I declared the Catholic Church the only religion of the Roman Empire, effectively ending for hundreds of years to come any real link between Judaism and the worldwide Church.

Lewis discovered for himself, in a world of very limited communication, that having been expelled from their own land of Israel, the Jews had also been forcibly removed at one time or another from every country they had settled in, including his own. And atrocities had been committed on these people who, parts of the Church began to teach, had been the 'Christ-killers' of the New Testament. He began to compile a list of events as best he could from his sources:

1020   Jews said to be banished from England by Canute.
1066   Jews return to England.
1189   The Jews massacred in London on the coronation day of Richard I, at the instigation of the Priests.
1190   500 Jews besieged in York Castle by the mob. They cut each other's throats to avoid falling into the hands of their bloodthirsty enemies.
1204   Jews of both sexes imprisoned, their eyes or teeth plucked out, and numbers inhumanly butchered by

King John.

1262   700 Jews are slain in London, because a Jew had made a Christian pay him more than 2s. a week as interest on a loan of 20s.

1269   Statute that no Jew should own a freehold.

1278   Jews accused of clipping coin, hundreds hanged and quartered.

1290   All Jews banished from England; and for two centuries cruelly pillaged and persecuted in France.

1348   A fatal distemper raging in Europe, Jews are accused of poisoning the springs and numbers massacred etc. etc.

By the time he got to the year 1665 he would have found the Jews had been banished from England for nearly three hundred years and were invited back by Oliver Cromwell for what can only be seen as mainly economic reasons. And in nearly another three hundred years Lewis could not know that over six million would be murdered throughout Europe under the Nazi regime. One and a half million of them would be children.

Of course, Lewis was aware of the dark and bloody deeds carried out, often in the name of religion, throughout history involving people being removed from the country they called home. The African slave trade continued even in Lewis's own day, forcibly removing people from their own land into slavery overseas, never to return.[23] What made the Jews so different to millions of others who suffered exile, deportation and slaughter?

---

[23] The Abolition of Slavery Act finally came into force in 1807 when Lewis was thirty-five.

That the world held the Jews in abhorrence seems to set them apart from any other persecuted people through the centuries. This abhorrence was, and still is, beyond the hatred and conflict which has motivated so much killing in the world. Abhorrence of the Jews would allow most of the world to stand by while millions of Jewish men, women and children were taken from their homes one by one with a view to destroying every last one of them in what would be called the *Shoah*, the Holocaust. Not just the chance tragic victims of total war, like so many, but part of a plan of total destruction with no chance of escape, no option to surrender.

Years later, in the old Jewish cemetery in Prague Lewis would begin to understand.

Chapter 6

"It seems odd, that certain men who talk so much of what the Holy Spirit reveals to themselves, should think so little of what he has revealed to others."

Charles H. Spurgeon

In 1805 Lewis and Mary had another son, Albert, born the same year as Nelson's great sea victory at Trafalgar. Their first child, Lewis, had died in 1804 and a daughter, Drusilla, was born on 28th May the same year. Now they were four and the Way's needed a bigger home, like most young families.

Lewis had been born in London but grew up in the idyllic setting of Denham Place, Buckinghamshire, lying east of the Chiltern Hills in the Colne Valley. His father, Benjamin,[24] had acquired the seventeen hectare (42 acre) estate in 1742 and it would remain in the family until 1920. But, as the second son, Lewis would not inherit it.

Today Denham House is a grade 1 listed building without general public access and is probably most easily viewed in the distance across the lake from the A412 Slough to Watford road. A kilometre-long red-brick wall, three metres high with security cameras forms part of the estate

---

[24] Benjamin Way (1740-1808)

boundary and does not encourage casual visitors. But it is easy to imagine the young Lewis Way and his many siblings running, playing and riding around the vast grounds, far from the worldly cares that awaited them.

Lewis had inherited a very large, though not entirely unexpected, fortune from his namesake John Way which, according to the wording of the will he was free to use for "his own proper use and benefit."[25] Legally it seems Lewis could spend the fortune as he liked, but there was at least an implied condition, which he always acknowledged and John Way's former solicitor, Andrew Edge, affirmed some years later in a statement dated January 27th, 1819 written at Stansted House, the home of Lewis Way:

"As far as my memory serves, Mr Lewis Way's expression of the Testator's meaning, declared to him previous to his decease, was the bequest made to him was the gift of God's providence, and should be used to the Glory of God."

Lewis, as a lawyer and a Christian, needed to be conscious of this condition as he sought a new home for his growing family. He had looked at a number of properties including the very attractive Trumpeters' House, on the Thames at Richmond. But Lewis turned it down and it was bought by the Earl and Countess of Yarmouth.

---

[25] "And first I (John Way) revoke the devise and bequest in my said will to the Revd Gregory Syndercombe of the residue of my personal estate and effects and do hereby give and devise the said residue of my said personal estate and effects unto Lewis Way of Boswell Court Esquire to and for his own proper use and benefit...."

About the same time in 1805 the magnificent Stansted Park near the city of Chichester, West Sussex, came on the market.[26] The auction took place at Garraway's Coffee-House, London[27] on Tuesday 21st May 1805 and Way purchased it for £173,000 ($280,260).[28] This was over half of Lewis's inherited fortune and was equivalent to at least five million pounds today though the property is actually valued at about thirty million pounds ($48,600,000) in real terms.

Daughter Drusilla, who was only one year old at the time apparently recalled many years later:

"Our father had a desire to purchase it [the Trumpeters' House] *happier perhaps than the large, beautiful Stansted, but then it seemed too moderate a villa for John Way's heir!"*[29]

Whether Lewis felt that way about his role as John Way's heir we cannot be sure, but he did indeed buy the Stansted property and spent a further £1,200 ($1,944) on deer for the 1,750 acres of glorious parkland. To get some idea of the size of Lewis's new home it could comfortably contain six of the top UK theme parks plus Disneyland, California![30]

---

[26] Today Stansted is a Grade II listed country house set on a 1,750-acre estate within the South Downs National Park.

[27] A Turkish style coffee house in St Michael's Alley, near the Royal Exchange, the first in London.

[28] *Enchanted Forest, The Story of Stansted in Sussex*, The Earl of Bessborough with Clive Aslet, 1984 p. 64

[29] *The Ways of Yesterday*, A. M. W. Stirling, 1930

[30] Alton Towers 500 acres, Thorpe Park 500, Legoland Windsor 150, Blackpool Pleasure Beach 42, Drayton Manor 280, Chessington World of Adventures 128.5, Disneyland California 85 = 1685.5 acres (682 hectares).

Lewis was faced with some big choices. If he was to comply with the spirit of the inheritance that the money should be used "to the Glory of God" he could either give it all, or most of it, to a good cause, which probably meant the Church at that time, or he could form an institution in his own name for his own cause. Unfortunately Lewis didn't have a particular cause at the time and he couldn't see the point of letting the Church deal with it because John Way could easily have done that himself in his will. Clearly John Way had expected Lewis to achieve what *he* had failed to establish in his lifetime and called:

"....an Eleemosynary or other Charitable Religious Society or Institution, and to found it with Church and landed Property suitable thereto...."

That had been John's stated ambition but he had never quite achieved it, so he had passed the onerous task on to Lewis. Perhaps John never had the entrepreneurial gifts that would be required to see it through. Lewis Way did have the gifts, or would acquire them, but for now he would invest half the money in a single property, raise his family there, at Stansted, and literally wait on the Lord.

The next six years, 1805-1811, would be spent planning his new chapel at Stansted and pursuing his eschatological Bible studies. Their son Albert would be born in the early summer of 1805, a brother to Drusilla and a much longed for son following the early death of young Lewis. Still only twenty-five, Mary settled easily into the life of mother and lady of the manor at Stansted. She could deal with the wealth and the power that went with it but she had been content in her earlier days, according to Lewis, to simply

37

"turn an old muslin petticoat into a short walking skirt." A practical lady, she would rule the house with the ease that came with her upbringing but clearly laced with humour and Christian love. She was much loved, both above and below stairs in the clearly defined social world of the early nineteenth century household of Stansted Park.

Lewis himself had signed up with the influential John Venn's[31] so-called Clapham Sect, an Anglican Evangelical group based in Clapham near London, whose leading light was William Wilberforce the slavery abolitionist. The Claphamites or Saints, as some called them, would play a major part in the final downfall of industrial scale slave trading. But the philanthropic and humanitarian works of the society spread much further and wider into all areas of society, especially the poorer classes and, although Lewis was sympathetic to the many worthy causes supported by the society, and contributed some of his wealth, he was most attracted by their teaching about the "end times" when Jesus would return in glory after a thousand years of worldwide moral improvement.

According to their understanding of the Bible, especially chapter 20 of the Revelation or Apocalypse, it would be the role of these upper class Evangelicals to take the lead in the evangelisation of the entire world, courtesy of the British Empire and, in particular, the entire Jewish people who were expected to be in place in the Holy Land ready and waiting for the Messiah Jesus, *their* Messiah, to return. Needless to say, the Roman Catholics would be left to their own devices with, according to many Protestant

---

[31] John Venn (1793-1813) rector of the Holy Trinity Church, Clapham.

Evangelicals at the time, little chance of surviving the wrath to come.[32]

All this would happen during a thousand year period, the end of which may not have been far off. This view of the future of the world was known as Postmillennialism because Jesus was expected to appear *after* a thousand years of successful evangelisation in preparation for his return. Such an optimistic view might seem today to be a little unreal and even bizarre but they really believed it and acted on it. This fallen world would pick itself up by its own scientific bootstraps in the strength of the Gospel and the power of the Holy Spirit. This literally 'apocalyptic' scenario was driven by the belief that they could interpret the 'signs of the times' referred to by Jesus in Matthew 16:2-3[33] and drew its authority from Jesus's statement following his resurrection and recorded in Matthew 24:14:

"......and this gospel of the kingdom will be preached in the whole world as a testimony to all nations, and then the end will come."

That indeed was at the heart of the Christian faith. Jesus had died in fulfilment of the Old Testament Jewish

---

[32] The Catholic Church rejects Postmillennialism and Premillenialism and is broadly Amillennial. See *Catechism of the Catholic Church 676, 1997.*

[33] [Jesus] replied, "When evening comes, you say, 'It will be fair weather, for the sky is red,' and in the morning, 'Today it will be stormy, for the sky is red and overcast.' You know how to interpret the appearance of the sky, but you cannot interpret the signs of the times. Matthew 16:2-3 NIV

prophesies, he *was* עמנואל, Emmanuel[34], 'God with us' (Matthew 1:23), the perfect 'once for all' sacrifice for sin. He is resurrected and promises to return to Judge the world. So far so good, but people wanted to know when in the future this would all happen. It wasn't enough, apparently, just to 'be prepared'. And so Lewis aligned himself with what would be called the Postmillennialists, working tirelessly to bring about a world based on Christian ethics, fit to present to the Messiah when he returned at the end of the thousand year programme.

Such an ambition, however faith-based and sincere, could probably only exist in the quasi-theocratic atmosphere of early 19th century England. This optimistic self-help theology began to crumble during the Great War of 1914-18 and all but disappeared amid the horrors of the Second World War and the Holocaust. Lewis Way would not live to see this further decline of mankind but would later reject Postmillennialism anyway, along with any belief that mankind would progress spiritually of its own volition. Lewis wrote:

"As secular advancement corrupted the simplicity of the spiritual character, a supremacy of man's invention was substituted for the sovereignty of Christ."[35]

He would later move to a Premillennial position anticipating Jesus' return *before* his thousand year rule on earth:

---

[34] Isaiah 7 and 8, Matthew 1:22-23
[35] *Palingenesia. The World to Come*, Lewis Way, 1822, To the reader.

"......they shall live again, and thus with Christ a thousand years partake his personal millennial reign!"[36]

Lewis would never subscribe to the so-called Amillennial view held by most Catholics and many Anglicans that the thousand years referred to in Revelation 20 was a symbolic number not meant to be taken literally. They believed the millennium represented a very long period of time and was in fact the 'Age of the Church' that we are still living in today. In his epic poem of 35,479 words, or what he calls a "didactic essay," *Palingenesia,* Lewis writes:

"There are who deem such period took its rise in days of sainted Helena, or reign of Trinobantian Constantine, when first a Christian monarch sat on Caesar's throne."[37]

Lewis rejects the doctrine on the grounds that Satan had not been bound during this period as prophecy required. He roamed at large, in his opinion, during such unhappy events as the Crusades and the Inquisition.

But for the studious, academic Lewis Way the day was approaching when his ministry would become clear. And so it was that a brief incident on a journey from Exmouth in East Devon would give him an almost Pauline vision of *his* role in the things to come. At last he would have a cause to fight for and a banner to raise.

---

[36] *Ibid.*, Book VII, p. 229
[37] *Ibid,* Book II, p. 38

Chapter 7

If you will it, it is no dream.

Theodor Herzl

A few miles outside Exmouth on the road to Exeter, now the A376, you turn right onto Summer Lane at Courtlands Cross to discover one of the most exciting, and quite magical, small houses in the whole of England. *A la Ronde*, named for its more or less round shape, though it's more of a sixteen-sided hexadecagon, looks down on the Exeter road and across the River Exe estuary to medieval Kenton, the Starcross Yacht Club and the distant sandy beach of Dawlish Warren.

Here lived the cousins Parminter, Jane and Mary[38] who, being comfortably off and having inherited a fortune from Jane's wine merchant father set up home here in 1795 and built *A la Ronde*, having spent the ten years from 1784 touring France, Italy, Germany and Switzerland by way of an extended Grand Tour. They filled the place with almost banal souvenirs which, alongside musical instruments, beautiful books, myriad seashells and *objets d'art* created a most comfortable, if slightly eccentric, homely atmosphere which still exists today[39].

---

[38] Jane Parminter (1750–1811), Mary Parminter (1767–1849)
[39] *A la Ronde* is owned today by the National Trust

The house, with its pointed thatched roof and fairy-tale bright red diamond shaped windows, was a model of ecological correctness for the time. It was designed for the ladies by Commander John Lowder to attract sunlight as it crossed from east to west and the cousins would move round some of the twenty rooms, connected by sliding doors and end their busy day in the oval western tearoom.

Jane Parminter died in 1811. Her sister Elizabeth had passed away in 1791 before work started on *A la Ronde.* Mary would continue to live there until her death in 1849.

Many stories surrounded the lives of the two cousins, some true, some not so true. Although not reclusive they did keep themselves to themselves in later life even having their own non-conformist chapel built in order not to travel to Exmouth for Sunday worship. The chapel, still there to this day, has its own horizontal pipe organ and bears the inscription:

"Some point in view - We all pursue"

which was a reference to their deep interest in the future of the Jewish people and their return to the Land of Israel as well as their own philanthropic work among the maiden ladies of the small local Jewish community.

One of the stories that circulated after the death of Jane referred to the so-called 'oaks of *A la Ronde.*' It was said that she had declared prophetically in her will that the oak trees at *A la Ronde* would stand until the Jews, some of them at least, would return to Palestine in boats made from the very same oak. This prophecy is not borne out by sight of her actual probated will but that is the story Lewis Way received as he rode past their home one cold winter's day in 1811 on his way back to his wife's family estate up the road at Grange.

As they rode past, conscious of the seventeen mile journey ahead and the oncoming winter darkness, his companion told Lewis some of the stories surrounding the two maiden ladies and the alleged declaration regarding the Jews. It may well be that something like this was on Jane Parminter's mind in her later years but she never got round to incorporating it in her will even if she had such thoughts. But it was enough for Lewis to take the information as true and providential as well as a sign that he should pursue his growing interest in the Jewish roots of Christianity.

Something had touched the heart and perhaps the soul of Lewis Way and like John Wesley in 1738 he had felt his "heart strangely warmed" by this simple and singular experience. This was the catalyst that would move Lewis forward and transport him to a new place, where God could use him, however apocryphal the Parminter story may have been.

When he returned to London Lewis made enquiries as to whether any organisation existed for encouraging the long promised return of the Jews to the Land of Israel and their recognition of Jesus as the equally long-awaited Messiah. He discovered that a society had been formed two years earlier, in 1809, called the London Society for Promoting

Christianity Amongst the Jews[40], for just such a purpose, and they were seriously short of funds. In that same year William Wilberforce presided at the third anniversary meeting of the Society and a further link was established in Lewis's mind with the Clapham Sect, described in the Society's centennial history[41] as:

"A company of choice spirits, Evangelical Churchmen, who periodically met at [Henry] Thornton's house on Clapham Common."

By 1813, at the London Society's anniversary meeting chaired by Lord Dundas at Freemasons Hall in London, Lewis himself was a speaker along with such worthies as Wilberforce, Charles Simeon and Henry Thornton.

In 1815 Sir Thomas Baring, Bart, MP, became President of the Society but when he discovered the extent of the Society's debt he prepared to withdraw his support. Happily Lewis would save the day and bankrolled the Society to the tune £10,000 ($16,200), which would save them from sinking and help them keep afloat for the next two hundred years.

"What was my surprise," wrote Baring, *"when, at our first meeting, I found the Society's debts and liabilities exceeded £14,000. I told him (Mr Way), on this discovery, that I must withdraw myself from it, that I never could consent to connect myself with a society in debt, and that I saw no remote probability of its relieving itself from its difficulties. Now mark*

---

[40] Today called the Church's Ministry Among Jewish People (CMJ)
[41] *The History of the London Society For Promoting Christianity Amongst the Jews from 1809 to 1908*, Rev. W.T. Gidney M.A., 1908

what this great and good man did. He put a draft for 10,000 into my hand. The other 4,000 was soon raised, and the debts of the Society were at once discharged.[42]

Even so, according to W.T. Gidney in his 1908 history of the Society, Baring had been reluctant to take the money on behalf of the Society until he was assured of Lewis Way's long term commitment by showing that he had already left that amount in his will and this was not "a mere momentary impulse of benevolence":

Lewis assured him of his bequest and in response said, "Let me have the privilege in my lifetime of giving the money, and thus stepping forward to assist the Society in this hour of its extremity." It is recorded in the November 1816 accounts that Lewis was also humble enough to pay in the modest sum of £2 on behalf of a Mrs H. More. This may well have been the writer and abolitionist Hannah More.[43]

Sir Thomas Baring would occupy the position of President for thirty-three years from 1815 to his death in 1848.

Lewis is supposed to have said the work he was about to undertake, effectively the restoration of Israel, would require "more than the faith of Abraham, the perseverance of Moses, and the patience of Job!"[44] Lewis was to learn

---

[42] *The History of the London Society For Promoting Christianity Amongst the Jews from 1809 to 1908*, Rev. W.T. Gidney M.A., 1908 P. 47
[43] Hannah More (1745-1833)
[44] *The History of the London Society For Promoting Christianity Amongst the Jews from 1809 to 1908*, Rev. W.T. Gidney M.A., 1908 P. 47

more about the simple faith and the human weakness of those three Patriarchs and how God worked through their weakness rather than their strengths. Lewis's frailty and failure were also to be among the tools God would use to achieve his own restoration plans a hundred years after Lewis's death, in 1948. From the earliest days the Society had seen its aim as:

"........being for the extension and diffusion of Christianity amongst this ancient people, and not the conversion of the entire race, a consummation not to be expected during this dispensation."[45]

The story of his revelation on the road to Exeter would often be repeated within the Society over the years in ever growing, and glowing, terms as Lewis's reputation grew. When the simple will was eventually brought to light many years later in 1882 by Benjamin Bradley,[46] without the critical prophesy, it would cause some embarrassment to the Society and might have tarnished the memory of Lewis Way. It seemed as if reputations would tumble as the foundations of a whole evangelistic movement, The London Society, began, so it seemed, to be shaken. Today, the story might be creatively rehashed to reflect the truth without detracting from the genuine spirit of Lewis's revelation but in the early 19th century such 'spin' however sincere, would not be acceptable to the dogged and ultra-conscientious Mr Bradley even though the

---

[45] *The History of the London Society For Promoting Christianity Amongst the Jews from 1809 to 1908*, Rev. W.T. Gidney M.A., 1908 *p.* 34

[46] Benjamin Bradley, accountant of the London Society for Promoting Christianity Among the Jews.

Society did try to kill the story off with a fast admission of the error.

Benjamin Bradley also took the opportunity to bring to light, through the popular medium of pamphleteering, the social networking of the nineteenth century, many other perceived abuses and errors within the London Society. The wounds took a long time to heal but did, apparently, lead to some useful reforms. "God moves in a mysterious way, His wonders to perform" went a popular hymn of the time[47] and then, as now, Christians believed God works through human weakness and frailty to fulfil his own purposes in the long run.

Meanwhile, back in 1819, long before these revelations, the myth of *A la Ronde* was still popular, as was Lewis Way, and he would become a Vice President of the Society. In time he was to set out on an overland journey to Moscow for the Society with an appointment to meet Tsar Alexander I, Emperor of Russia. Russia was home to over two million Jews, more than enough perhaps for Miss Parminter's oak ships, but Lewis would not be deterred.

---

[47] *God Moves in Mysterious Ways*, William Cowper (1731–1800)

Chapter 8

"Do you know, the only people I can have a conversation with are the Jews? At least when they quote scripture at you they are not merely repeating something some priest has babbled in their ear. They have the great merit of disagreeing with nearly everything I say. In fact, they disagree with almost everything they say themselves. And most importantly, they don't think that shouting strengthens their argument."

Iain Pears, *The Dream of Scipio*

In 1816 Lewis Way had been ordained Deacon in the Church of England, becoming an Anglican priest in 1817. This, presumably, would give him more credibility among the important people he was beginning to associate with, but it also fulfilled his youthful ambition to enter the Church rather than take to the law as his father had wished.

The young family continued to grow although Charlotte Eliza had died in 1812 tragically within a month of her Baptism and was buried in the village of Stoughton, West Sussex. Lewis wrote these words in November 1813:

ON VISITING CHARLOTTE'S GRAVE

How short the time! how sure the power to save,
Behold! the font the passage to the grave;
How great the privilege! at once to go,
To bliss above, without offence below.
Glory be thine! Thou favoured child of grace;
The prize obtained, ere yet commenced the race;
Not length of days, but innocence thine age,
And life unspotted, all thy pilgrimage;
No staff thou needest, no chastising rod,
Thy peace unbroken, is the peace of God
Past understanding - for to such is given
Abundant entrance by the Lord of Heaven -
"His Name be hallow'd" o'er thy early tomb,
His will accomplished, and His kingdom come!"

Anna Mary, born in 1813, would survive to see the Franco-Prussian war. She died in 1881. Their third son Herman, named after Mary's father, died in 1816 aged two years but Olivia, born in 1816 would live well into the Victorian age, dying in 1888. Only one son would survive beyond childhood and that was Albert, born 1805 and living to see Baron Haussmann's renovation of his father's adopted city of Paris. Albert, a man of independent means, made a career for himself as an antiquarian, becoming founder of the Royal Archaeological Institute in London. He died in Cannes, France in 1874.

Two more children would follow, Catherine Louisa (1818-1906) and Georgiana Millicent (1820-1855), making six survivors out of the nine children born to Lewis and Mary.

In 1815 the chancel which Lewis had been adding to the chapel at Stansted was opened. The decoration reflected his memories of the chapel at his childhood home in Denham. On 28th May the same year the chapel, which is believed to be the only church in England with the Ten Commandments written in Hebrew on stone tablets on the wall, was consecrated by the Bishop of St. David's, Wales. It was completed in 1816 and a new age was about to begin for the Reverend Lewis Way.

But Lewis's dream of a college based at Stansted for potential Jewish missionaries who would go out into the world as believers in Jesus the Jewish Messiah, was on hold as he struggled with the options available to him, and those opposed to him.

He was torn between two major choices. He could set up a private college at Stansted using perhaps a whole wing of the building and still live with his family in the rest of the house. In that way he could pass the estate on to his surviving son Albert and his descendants while still maintaining the spirit of John Way's will, at least for a generation. But that choice had several disadvantages. Although it would keep the Stansted estate in the hands of his family Lewis would not be able to issue any formal qualifications to his students, no more than perhaps a certificate of attendance, and he could not be sure that his heirs would wish to maintain the house as a Hebrew college within the implied terms of John Way's will. On the other hand, if he applied for formal recognition as an academic institution he would have to hand the estate or, presumably, most of it to a Board of Trustees who would ensure continuity. The struggle would continue for several years as his uncle, Edward Cooke[48] threatened and cajoled him with his family duty and the government refused to establish a Hebrew College in England at any price.

Meanwhile, Lewis was preparing to get away from it all, on a journey to Russia which would take him much further and deeper than he had ever planned. The London Society was sending the Revd Benjamin Nehemiah Solomon to the Crimea in southern Russia in response to the Tsar Nicholas's Imperial Ukase allotting land to 'converted' Jews; Lewis would bankroll the project and meanwhile develop his own agenda for the future of European Jews by arranging a personal meeting with the Tsar.

Uncle Edward wrote bitterly to him in July 1817:

".....I have learnt that previous to your setting off for Russia you are preparing to convey to Trustees for Hebrew purposes the whole of your Stansted Property, Civil and Ecclesiastical, and to disinherit your Children."

But there was no immediate risk of Stansted becoming an institution or the children being turned out on the streets.

In the meantime Lewis would invite Jewish people who had shown an interest in the Christian faith to join him at his home at Stansted and share the benefits of his extensive Hebrew library and his own understanding of the

---

[48] The Right Hon. Edward Cooke (1755-1820), Under-Secretary in the Irish Military Department 1789-1795; and in the Civil Department 1796-1801; M.P. Leighlin 1790-1800.

embryonic Messianic movement. These potential so-called Hebrew Christians would, he hoped, recognise Jesus as their Messiah, learn the fundamental teachings of the Church and recognise the fulfilment of the Jewish Bible prophecies (the Old Testament) in Jesus. Generally these Hebrew Christians would be happy to integrate into local Christian churches.

It would not be until the mid-twentieth century that the term "Messianic Jews", with groups such as Jews for Jesus, would become popular. They would retain much of their Jewish culture, for example, using Hebrew names for New Testament Jewish characters who they thought had lost their "Jewishness" in Greek translation and Christian tradition. Jesus would become Yeshua; Mary would be Miriam and so on. In other words a much more Jewish religion, as it supposedly was in the first century.

Among the guests Lewis would take under his wing at Stansted prior to his departure for Russia were a number of less respectable Jewish enquirers who saw an opportunity to jump on the fashionable evangelistic gravy train. At one point he had sixteen Jewish guests at Stansted who may or may not have been genuine enquirers. Times were tough and free board and lodging was not to be sneezed at. After all, didn't Protestant King Henry IV convert to Roman Catholicism with the throwaway line, "Paris is worth a mass" in order to be King of France?

But one day a rumour began to circulate that Lewis Way was about to go bankrupt. Given his generosity and benevolence this might well have been true and so the sixteen would-be converts absconded with the library, the family silver and almost anything that wasn't nailed down. Jacob Josephson,[49] age thirty-five, probably the ringleader, was caught with stolen property and forged banknotes in his possession. He could easily have been hanged for such an offence but instead he was sentenced to fourteen years transportation. He would spend six months chained up in the ancient prison ships moored on the River Thames, the hulks, awaiting transportation by sea to Botany Bay, Australia.

It is tempting to be reminded of the good bishop in Victor Hugo's *Les Misérables* who, on finding Jean Valjean had been arrested for stealing his silver, refused to press charges and even offered him his silver candlesticks, a gift, which, he said, Valjean had forgotten. But this was, it must be said, a work of fiction, and any real-life offence connected with forgery was very severely punished in England and in France.[50] It's nice to think Lewis did put a word in for him because Jacob actually got off quite lightly, for the times!

He arrived in Sydney with 169 other convicts on 15th May 1818, a year after being sentenced, on the three-master convict ship *Neptune*. In October of that year he would open a jeweller's shop, his trade being a silversmith, in Pitt Street, Sydney. That was the practical reality of penal

---

[49] Jacob Josephson, born 21st April 1782 Breslau, Prussia (now Wroclaw Poland), died 6th December 1845 Marrickville Sydney, Australia

[50] According to a thirty franc bank note produced as late as 1927 forgery could be punished by hard-labour for life (*Le contrefacteur sera puni des forcés à perpétuité*).

colony life in New South Wales. He received a conditional pardon[51] on the 30th June 1820.

Jacob never returned to England and would have a colourful life in Australia. One of his sons would become Mayor of Marrickville, a suburb of Sydney, in 1901.

---

[51] Conditional Pardons were granted on condition that convicts did not return to England or Ireland.

Chapter 9

Lebisch: Rabbi! May I ask you a question?
Rabbi: Certainly, Lebisch!
Lebisch: Is there a proper blessing... for the Tsar?
*Rabbi: A blessing for the Tsar? Of course! May God bless and
keep the Tsar... far away from us!*

Joseph Stein, *Fiddler on the Roof*

Flying time from London to St Petersburg is about four-
and-a-half hours, less with a good tail wind. The GPS
recommended motoring route via Berlin and Warsaw is
1,735 miles (2,792 km). It should take 30 hours and 56
minutes, presumably with two drivers and some tea
breaks. In addition you could sail to St Petersburg, the
'Venice of the North', and then take a leisurely river cruise
down to Moscow.

There were not so many choices when planning a journey
to Russia's capital city in 1817 and for Lewis and his team
it would be more like two thousand miles as they would
have to chase the elusive Tsar to Moscow from their
original destination of St Petersburg. The French Emperor
Napoleon had made a disastrous trip to Moscow only five
years before, in 1812, having failed to occupy St
Petersburg, but then he, unlike Lewis, did not have a
personal introduction to the Tsar. The musical *Fiddler on
the Roof*, quoted above, is set in 1905 under Tsar Nicholas

II, sometimes known as Bloody Nicolas as a result of the anti-Semitic pogroms, but Lewis hopefully had an appointment with the more likeable Tsar Alexander I, who ruled Russia from 1801 to 1825 and was a friend to the Russian Jews, at least for the time being.[52]

Since his defeat at the Battle of Waterloo by the Duke of Wellington in 1815 Napoleon was no longer a threat to England or Russia and Lewis could set out in his custom-built carriage. This oversized stagecoach, pulled by two strong horses, was designed and built to withstand the worst roads of Northern Europe and Russia, had every modern convenience and seems to have been the 19th century equivalent of those six-wheeled American motorhomes.

On Saturday 9th of August 1817 they headed from a prayer meeting at Colchester in Essex to the port of Harwich to take the *paqueboat* to Hellevoetsluis in Holland and their first port of call at Rotterdam. Lewis clutched the pictures of his wife, Mary, and four children, Drusilla, Albert, Anna Mary, and Olivia. He had commissioned the paintings, which are now in the British Museum in London, from artist John Downman[53] especially for the trip, and he carried them carefully in a large red leather wallet. It is not hard to imagine him looking at them every

---

[52] Catherine II (1729-1796) had already exhibited a certain degree of liberality toward the Jews: and when Alexander succeeded to the throne, on the assassination of his father, Paul, in 1801, the liberal - or, rather, radical - disposition of the young ruler and of his advisers soon permeated all departments of the government and extended even to the public at large. *Jewish Encyclopaedia* 1906
[53] John Downman (1750-1824)

night as the long, uncomfortable journey took him further and further from them. The *Jewish Expositor*,[54] the monthly magazine of the London Society reported their departure on behalf of the newly formed Colchester Auxiliary Society:

The party embarked at Harwich on the 9th of August 1817. The weather was fine, the breeze favourable, and a rainbow appeared over the vessel as she sailed out of the harbour. Our hearts were animated with a fervent hope that this ship actually carried from our favoured shore the first swift messengers to a nation scattered and peeled.[55]

In 1610 the worthy Burghers of Rotterdam had welcomed a small number of Portuguese Jewish merchants who would form the foundation of the thriving community Lewis would meet two hundred years later. "I have visited all the synagogues, and conversed with most of the chief Rabbis from Rotterdam to Moscow," Lewis would later claim, his enthusiasm and commitment never failing as the ever courteous and inquisitive Jews of northern Europe entertained this extraordinary gentile *milord* from England.

Reform was in the air and new ideas flourished even in the conservative Jewish communities. 'Emancipation through assimilation' was seen by many as the way forward in the coming industrial age, the age of revolution. After all, Lewis must have thought, many of the Second Temple priests had listened and accepted Messiah Jesus, according

---

[54] *The Jewish Expositor, and Friend of Israel*, Volume II, 1817, p. 368
[55] Peeled. Probably from peel, a 16th century fortified house, suggesting they were ghettoised.

to *Acts 6:7*, why not the Chief Rabbis of his own time? Might not such a response be found even among the Orthodox in these 'end times'?

But Lewis does not seem to have fully taken into account, at this early stage, nearly two thousand years of enforced separation and distrust. Christianity had long been seen by most Jews as a 'foreign' religion with little or no connection to Judaism, especially after the destruction of the Second Temple and the *diaspora*. Judaism had long been seen by most gentile Christians as obsolete, no longer being connected to the Old Testament or indeed the equally Jewish New Testament except as a failed and superseded 'chosen people.' In 1934, four years before *Kristallnacht* the Czech journalist Egon Erwin Kisch would go to the heart of the Church's separation and the 'conversion' issue:

The Portuguese Synagogue [in Amsterdam] is not, for instance, like the Altneu Shul in Prague. In no way could it be described as a shabby, shivering, timorous meeting place for illegal immigrants - no, it is a splendid construction, a Jewish cathedral... The nave, supported by pillars of hewn granite, reaches to the heavens and resembles those churches in Iberia where Jews of yore were dragged in to hear sermons of conversion to Christianity, or to be forcibly baptized.[56]

Eighty per-cent of the 80,000 Jewish population of Amsterdam would be murdered in the Holocaust a few years later, but the great Portuguese Synagogue is still standing after 340 years, its red-brick walls towering like a

---

[56] Egon Erwin Kisch, *Emigrants: place of residence - Amsterdam*

citadel over the Muiderstraat. Lewis would visit the city on his journey and would arrange, with the support of Charles Simeon,[57] for the London Society to appoint and support a missionary to the Jews of Amsterdam.

The separation of Jew and Gentile had been seriously encouraged ever since the Roman Emperor Theodosius I, in the footsteps of his predecessor Constantine, effectively divorced the Church from her Jewish roots in AD 380.[58] Thus it was with Emperor Theodosius's decree which began:

"It is our desire that all the various nations which are subject to our Clemency and Moderation should continue to profess that religion which was delivered to the Romans by the divine Apostle Peter as it has been preserved by faithful tradition."

Theodosius himself had nothing personal against the Jews and even encouraged them to practice their separate religion. His real target was the pagan Romans who were prepared to destroy the newly founded Christian church, and very nearly did. Sadly, however, some lesser men would, in time, take advantage of the growing separation to impose their own views on the historical relationship between the Jewish people and the Church. The Jewish people were to become, in time, the "Christ killers."

But, like so many major events in Christian history, from Henry VIII's break with the Pope to Martin Luther's

[57] Charles Simeon (1759-1836). One of the founders of the London Society for Promoting Christianity Amongst the Jews (later CMJ).
[58] On 27 February 380 the State Church of the Roman Empire was established with the *Edict of Thessalonica*.

Reformation, ordinary people were not immediately affected. Far from it, their hard lives just went on and the church barely changed outside the major centres of power. And so, in the newly enlightened times of the nineteenth century the innocent message from Lewis Way, and so many others, was that although the Church had taken over now,[59] the Jews were very welcome to join their Jewish Messiah and his 'bride'[60] at the feast. But the reality was very much harder. The majority Jewish element in the early days of the Church had been alienated by the growing gentile leadership. The task of the Church now was really reconciliation and repentance, but it would take many years and the near destruction of the Jewish people before that would begin to happen in the wider Church, Catholic or Protestant.

It would begin in 1962 at the twenty-first Ecumenical Council of the Catholic Church, better known as Vatican II. A declaration was finally made that "the responsibility for Christ's death falls upon sinful mankind." In other words, both Jew and gentile. It further declared, "It is therefore unjust to call this people deicide or to consider it cursed by God."[61] Morris B. Abram president of the American Jewish Committee at the time concluded:

---

[59] Replacement Theology

[60] The Christian Church is sometimes referred to as the Bride of Christ.

[61] *Nostra Aetate - Declaration on the Relation of the Church with Non-Christian Religions* - Second Vatican Council, 1963-65

"Acceptance of this decree will make it impossible for anyone to instigate hatred for Jews and claim sanction or support in Christian teaching or dogma."[62]

Better late than never perhaps.

But for now, in the thriving Dutch port of Rotterdam, the adventure had only just begun, and Lewis was as convinced as ever that, with the help of the British Empire and the Tsar of Russia, the Jewish people would soon be on their way back to the land of Israel. He had acquired an introduction to the Tsar from his uncle, Edward Cooke,[63] an Old Etonian who happened to be the British Under-Secretary for Foreign Affairs at the time.

Of all the European leaders, Alexander I had the best relationship with the Jews. Whereas Napoleon had simply seen them as a potential French ally in the Middle East, Alexander truly recognised the Jewish people, in a brief window of enlightenment, as the root of the wild olive branch that was Christianity. He understood St Paul's oft-ignored question, and answer:

"Did they [the Jews] stumble so as to fall beyond recovery? Not at all! Rather, because of their transgression, salvation has come to the Gentiles to make Israel envious. But if their transgression means riches for the world, and their loss means riches for the Gentiles, how much greater riches will their full inclusion bring! (Romans 11:11-12)

---

[62] Comment on the first draft, *Decretum de Judaeis* (Decree on the Jews), reported in *America – The National Catholic Review*, 30th November 1963
[63] Edward Cooke (1755–1820)

The time was right. The bizarre little team of Charles Maberley, Lewis's secretary; the Revd Robert Cox of the London Society; Sultan Kategerry, interpreter and Tartar Prince; Benjamin Nehemiah Solomon, the first translator of the New Testament into Yiddish, who would work among the Jews of the Crimea, and, last but not least, a servant named John, known to the children at Stansted as "the Duke of Puddledock" headed off to meet the most powerful man in the world.

From Rotterdam and Amsterdam they pressed on to Hanover and eventually the great walled city of Berlin, capital of Prussia, just a decade after its short occupation by Napoleon in 1807. It was here in Berlin that the great journey ground to a halt as Benjamin Nehemiah Solomon met with one of the greatest challenges of his Christian life.

Benjamin was born of Jewish parents in Lemberg, Poland[64] in 1791 and would, in time, become a rabbi. In 1814 he arrived in London and gave his life to Messiah Jesus through the ministry of Joseph Frey,[65]founder of the London Society. He would eventually be ordained in the Church of England. Benjamin had a wife and two children whom he wanted to bring to England and he had promised not to put any pressure on her, or the children, to give up their Jewish faith. He had understood this

---

[64] Lemberg is now known as Lviv and finds itself in western Ukraine today. Lviv was the setting for the 2011 Polish film *In Darkness* which records the destruction of the Jews in that city and the ultimate heroism of the gentile Pole Poldek Socha.

[65] Joseph Samuel Christian Frederick Frey (born Joseph Levi) (1771–1850)

would be acceptable to her family but, to his great surprise, he was met in Berlin by her enraged father who told him in no uncertain terms that he would have to divorce his Jewish daughter if he wished to continue in the Christian faith.

The father-in-law had travelled from the port of Hamburg where Benjamin's wife and children were living at the time, perhaps *en route* to England to stay with Alice Way and await her husband's plans for them. It is not hard to imagine the conflict in his heart. With Lewis Way's permission and blessing Benjamin travelled to Hamburg with their companion Revd Cox in the hope of convincing his wife of his sincerity. He asked her and entreated her tearfully to stay with him without his giving up his faith in Messiah Jesus, but to no avail. After eight or ten days Benjamin became convinced that there could be no reconciliation. *The Missionary Register* of December 1817 solemnly reports it thus:

That a godly Jewess should consent to cohabit with a Christian, and especially a Meshumad *(an Apostate Jew) was a thing not to be heard of in Israel!*[66]

And so the sad ceremony duly took place at Altona[67] in the presence of three Rabbis and "other suitable Jewish witnesses." With a heavy heart Benjamin Nehemiah Solomon returned to Berlin, comforted by Jesus's promise in his *King James Bible* that:

---

[66] *The Missionary Register*, December 1817, p. 507
[67] Altona, Germany, now part of Hamburg on the estuary of the river Elbe.

"....every one that hath forsaken houses, or brethren, or sisters, or father, or mother, or wife, or children, or lands, for my name's sake, shall receive an hundredfold, and shall inherit everlasting life..." Matthew 19:29

Lewis meanwhile was paying a visit to Martin Luther's city of Wittenberg, seventy miles from Berlin, to witness the three hundredth anniversary of the Reformation. Solomon in a brief time of solitude writes a poignant letter to Mary Way in England:

Berlin 4th October 1817

My Dear Mrs Way,

I think I have promised in my last to you, to write again from Berlin - if however I have not been true to my engagement during the whole of Mr Way's stay in this place, it has not been from forgetfulness or from an indisposition to correspond with you - I myself, my dear Madam, have been of late put to many trials and great afflictions which if I should attempt to relate to you would be too much for me – our dear friend Mr Hawtrey will probably inform you of the whole, and at present I can but tell you in short, that I was obliged to go from here to Hamburg, where I have but seen my dear family once more, and have been put to the pains of separating from them, at least from my beloved wife by a final separation. It is now that I have experienced in a peculiar manner ended, what it is to leave wife and children for Christ and his Gospel's sake and to forsake one or the other was my only alternative - you will be able from this to form some idea of the trying situation in which I have been and still am after all is finished - it is my only comfort to be convinced that it is for the Lord's sake I have done it, and to remember that I have done all a father and a husband and a Christian could do to prevent the divorce but the Lord's will be done and not mine has been my motto, and may it be ours till the day of our departure out of this vale of tears.

He goes on to report on Lewis's health and recent events, but it is clear he welcomes the opportunity to share his great sadness with the sympathetic and sensitive Mary back in the comfortable world of Stansted.

Chapter 10

"The army, like a herd of cattle run wild and trampling underfoot the fodder which might have saved it from starvation, was disintegrating and perishing with every day it remained in Moscow."

Leo Tolstoy, *War and Peace*

Although the team would pass through several countries, or states, language was not a serious problem in 19th century Europe. Long before English became a universal language, French was the *lingua franca* of educated people in Europe and the official language of diplomacy. Catherine the Great had introduced the language to the Russian aristocracy and it was widely used in Moscow and St Petersburg. It lingered pretentiously in middle-class England through to the 1950s in phrases like, *pas devant les domestiques*, not in front of the servants! Lewis Way's French was fluent, if a bit academic, as was the rest of the team....all except the poor Revd Cox. It had not, apparently, been picked up at interview that Mr Cox didn't actually speak French! He was sent home, but not before they reached Moscow.

Anti-Semitism, the scourge of Eastern Europe was, for the moment, out of fashion, *alt modisch*, in Berlin, especially among the students of the Royal Frederick William University, now the Humboldt University on Unter den

Linden, which had opened its doors in 1810 to both Jewish and gentile students. Even in liberal England Jews and other dissenters were not allowed to take degrees at Oxford and Cambridge until the 1870s, but Jewish undergraduates were welcomed at Berlin without any need to deny their faith. The Jews of Prussia had reluctantly been granted partial emancipation in 1812 as the state prepared for its struggle with Napoleon, but they still could not hold any official state office.

Their stay in Berlin would prove to be productive. Lewis's persistence in obtaining an audience with the Tsar had paid off. His Uncle Edward had at first been reluctant to use his influence for such a fanciful scheme, but, having persisted, doors were opening for Lewis at the very highest level. No return to the Land of Israel would take place without the support of kings and emperors. But Lewis would not meet the Chief Rabbi in this city; Zvi Hirsch, Chief Rabbi of Berlin, had died in 1800 and had not been replaced.

It is said that Rabbi Hirsch had once been asked the following question by the Duke of Manheim, "Is it not written in the Torah that your God is a jealous and vengeful God, whereas ours is one of love and goodness?" The Rabbi replied, "I am in complete agreement: Our God took jealousy and vengeance upon Himself, and He left us love and forgiveness, whereas yours took love and forgiveness, and gave you jealousy and vengeance." Lewis should have met him.

It seems the Ways of Denham had rubbed shoulders with royalty in the past when King George III visited the family and took a shine to Elizabeth Ann, Lewis's mother. Now the struggling lawyer turned landowner would use his court contacts, in this case Sir George Rose, British Ambassador to Prussia, to obtain an introduction to the Crown Prince Frederick William. The Prince, who would eventually become King Frederick William IV of Prussia, took a great interest in Lewis's mission to the Jews and would remain his friend for many years. Like Tsar Alexander I the prince had an interest in all things mystical and apocalyptic so Lewis was never short of opportunities to share his own Biblical vision of the future. But even now perhaps a new dream was forming, to improve the lot of the Jews of Europe, especially in the East, to the mutual advantage of Jew and gentile and within the context of long-term Biblical prophecy. The return of Jesus might not be so imminent after all.

On Thursday 6th November 1817, Lewis and his companions left Berlin and headed east towards Poznan and then north to Torun in modern day Poland, now in a much smaller carriage with two enormous wheels that curved outwards, made especially for driving on the wasteland and beaches of the barren Baltic coast. Onward and upward, the five intrepid men and their baggage headed north to Riga, capital of Latvia. Lewis, Maberley and the Sultan left their wheeled carriage at Riga along with Revd Cox and Benjamin Solomon, and continued the journey to St Petersburg by sledge as winter set in. Lewis leaves us a colourful description of this transport in a letter to his mother:

"The winter being now set in, wheels are no longer useful, so we left the carriage and the Jew[68] with Mr Cox at Riga, and Sultan, Maberley and I have passed two delightful days travelling faster than an English Mail in a Sledge.

It has a body of panels like a barouche, with a door, a drop blind to keep off snow, a place where the Swagger sits smoking his pipe, a wing or fin projecting to prevent overturn, a board held up by iron for footmen to stand on when used for pleasure, and a string by which the footmen hold. This is drawn by three horses abreast, and they gallop as hard as they can as far as from London to Windsor, or Denham, stopping only for snaps. This is done by moonlight or starlight just as well as by daylight of which there is now but little. The thermometer stands at about 20 degrees below Freezing on the outside, at summer heat, above 70, in the inside. When we come to an Inn we are sure to find the temperature the same, as the fireplaces, here called ovens, are always hot, and you wake and get up in the same heat as you lie down on what is called a bench in England and a bed in Russia!

I now sleep in my own blanket, with the same clothes over me as I wear in the carriage. I have not yet had recourse to fur, except one little animal, the skin of which I wear under my shirt as a warm friend, two of the legs go round my neck, and the other two are held as a stummager[69] below - under this is a woolen waistcoat and over the shirt a leather waistcoat then a common waistcoat - two great coats and a Polish silk pelisse stuffed with wadding. It is surprising how completely the elements are brought into subjection! for, after all, when the air is too cold to breathe it is brought through a pipe of burning tobacco, and then is better than summer. . . . I have not yet tasted tallow candle, except in soup. . . . You see I live in a cradle and my chief food is

---

[68] Benjamin Nehemiah Solomon (1790-?)

[69] See OED Stomacher or stumager

rusks! ... We hope to reach our destination at St. Petersburg in two days."

Lewis arrived in the Imperial city of St Petersburg, the capital of Russia at the time, on 11th December 1817 with the Sultan and secretary Maberley. He collected his mail and headed for the Tsar's residence, the beautiful Winter Palace clutching his letter of introduction. The palace, designed by Francesco Bartolomeo Rastrelli, had been finished in 1764. It would be partly destroyed by fire 1837, and restored in 1839. The interior was, and still is, magnificent. The Crown Jewel Room contained the Imperial Regalia; the sceptre alone valued at over two million roubles, on which was, and still is mounted the celebrated Orlov diamond of 189.62 metric carats; the beautiful Imperial Crown (another million roubles), and many other objects of enormous value, now in the Moscow Kremlin. In the picture gallery were all the portraits of the Romanovs from the Patriarch Philarete Nikitich, father of Mikháil, the first of the Romanov Tsars.

The fairy-tale splendour of the Winter Palace, set like a white and azure wedding cake between the frozen river *Neva* and the snow-clad icing of Palace Square, must have left Lewis Way disappointed when he found the Emperor was not at home. The Imperial Standard wasn't flying and his Majesty had left for Moscow. Lewis would eventually have two meetings, he calls them interviews, with Alexander in Russia.

The first meeting would now be in what Lewis calls the 'new'[70] Kremlin palace in Moscow[71] rather than the Winter Palace in Petersburg. When they finally arrived in Moscow the city was still being rebuilt. Lewis describes it as "half-rebuilt, half ruins." In 1813 a great building programme had been started following the near destruction of the mostly wooden city by fire during its short occupation by Napoleon's *Grande Armée*. Rebuilding the Bolshoi theatre and the University were the priorities and much restoration work was required in the Kremlin, but the work still remained unfinished. When the French army was forced to retreat in 1812 the city had been almost totally destroyed, either intentionally or as a result of multiple uncontrolled fires; a Pyrrhic victory for Russia but a disaster for Napoleon and France. Alexander I[72] was Emperor of Russia from 23rd March 1801 to 1st December 1825. He was the grandson of Catherine the Great and reluctantly came to the throne through her machinations.

He was, like Lewis Way, a dreamer of dreams, but did not, or could not, always see them through. The Anglican clergyman with a heart for Israel and the man who defeated Napoleon Bonaparte and chased him back to Paris would become friends, but like Henry V and Falstaff,

---

[70] *Memorandum of an interview with his Imperial Majesty Alexander Emperor of all the Russias* – 1818 - Parkes Library Special Collections, University of Southampton, MS 85 Papers of Lewis Way

[71] Also later known as the 'Small Nicolas Palace' it was built by Matvey Kazakov in 1775-1776 as the Archbishop's House and converted into a palace in 1817-1818. It was only small in comparison to the Grand Kremlin Palace built from 1837 to 1849. The Small Nicolas Palace was demolished in 1929.

[72] Born Aleksandr Pavlovich

Henry II and Becket, Henry VIII and Thomas Moore or even Queen Victoria and Mr Brown, emperors and empresses have duties above their dreams and all these friendships would eventually give way to political reality. The Tsar shared Lewis's dream for the return of the Jews to their Fatherland, but he also had to deal with his neighbour, the crumbling but powerful Ottoman Empire which was not so keen to welcome back its old neighbour Israel.

In terms of religion Tsar Alexander is often seen as being a confused mystic under the unhealthy influence of the Russian visionary Barbara Juliane Krüdener,[73] but by the time he met Lewis Way in 1818 he had invited the more conservative evangelical British Bible Society to Russia to make the Bible available to his people in their own languages. The Russian Bible Society would soon be formed with generous imperial aid. By this time Alexander had fallen out with the visionary Krüdener because, in the way of absolute monarchs, he would not accept her visions for his future. He wanted a different vision. This change of heart probably came about under the influence of his confidant Prince Gallitzin prior to the arrival of Lewis Way.

In the American *Methodist Magazine*[74] for December 1819 a correspondent named simply R.F. wrote a letter to the editor about Tsar Alexander I and Prince Gallitzin under the heading *Anecdote of the Emperor Alexander*. It may be worth reproducing in full as the same report appears in an

---

[73] Barbara Juliane Krüdener (1764-1824)
[74] Published for The Methodist Episcopal Church in the United States

unidentified newspaper cutting in the Lewis Way archives at the University of Southampton but with the additional phrase, "....and a variety of circumstances combine to show that he became truly converted to Christ."

To the Editors of the Methodist Magazine.

Sir,

It has been said of the Christian religion, that "Kings shall be its fostering fathers, and Queens its nursing mothers." How fully this has been verified it is unnecessary to relate, or produce arguments to prove, as few, if any, deny it. It is, however, with great pleasure that we see the mighty Emperor of all the Russias listed under its banners, and lending his powerful aid to spread through his vast dominions the known edge of those Holy Oracles which are at once the foundation of the whole fabrick of it, and the only sure guide to a perfect acquaintance with it, and enjoyment of it. It has often been asked, "How the Russian court, formerly the most licentious on the Continent, should now be so zealous in promoting the objects of the Bible Society?" A few particulars, lately come to my knowledge, upon this subject, may not be uninteresting to your readers. When Alexander came to the throne, few Bibles were to be found in his empire, and still fewer readers of them. The forms of religion were indeed practised, but its influence was not felt, and the term Bible-reader was only used in derision, or as an epithet of contempt. A high place in the church and state (it is said the highest) became vacant by the death of the person who had filled it. The Emperor appointed his favourite and friend, the Prince Gallitzin, who had been and was his constant companion, in all his pursuits of pleasure, and who at first refused it, on the plea of his entire ignorance of religion; but this objection was over-ruled by the Emperor, who considered it of no weight. The Prince, on his first interview with the venerable Archbishop Platoff, requested him 'to point out some book, which would give him a concise view of the Christian religion. The Archbishop, rather surprised at the

Prince's professed ignorance, recommended the Bible. The Prince said he could not think of reading that book. "Well," replied the Archbishop, "that is the only book there is, or ever will be, that can give you a correct view of the Christian religion." "Then I must remain ignorant of it - reading the Bible is out of the question!" was his reply. The words, however, of the venerable Platoff remained upon his mind, and he shortly afterwards privately bought and read the Bible. The effects were soon visible. He was not known to be a "Bible-reader," but his manners were treated with contempt. Everyone was disturbed now by the threatened invasion by the French - Galitzin was not so. His companions were astonished. Was he become a traitor to his prince? It was impossible, his loyalty was undoubted. At this important crisis he thought it his duty to acquaint the Emperor with the rock on which he rested unmoved at the threatened danger. He requested an interview; it was granted. The invasion was naturally the first subject of conversation; and next, as closely connected with it, the Prince's conduct. The Emperor demanded upon what principle he remained calm and unmoved, in the midst of universal alarm? The Prince drew from his pocket a small Bible, and held it towards the Emperor, who putting his hand out to receive it, it by some means or other fell, and opened at the 91st Psalm. "O that your Majesty would, seek this retreat," said the Prince, as he read the words of the Psalm. They separated. A day was appointed for public prayer. The minister who preached took for his subject the 91st Psalm. The Emperor, surprised, inquired of the Prince if he had mentioned the circumstance that occurred at the interview, who assured him that he had not named it. A short time after, the Emperor having a few minutes leisure, and perhaps feeling the necessity of Christian support, sent for his chaplain, to read the Bible to him in his tent. He came, and began the 91st Psalm. "Hold," said the Emperor, "who told you to read that?" "God," replied the chaplain. "How!" exclaimed Alexander. "Surprised at your message," continued the chaplain, "I fell upon my knees before my God, and besought him to teach my weak lips what to speak. I felt that 'part of the Holy Word, which I have begun to read, clearly pointed out to me. Why your Majesty interrupted me, I know not." These circumstances made a deep impression on the Emperor's mind, and after the memorable battle of Leipsiche wrote to the Empress, (a virtuous and pious Princess, to whom he had been married soon after his accession, but from whom he was a short time afterwards separated) to come and see what the Lord had done for him! and since which they have lived in the strictest bond of union and connubial happiness.

With congratulations for the past and best wishes for your future success, I beg to subscribe myself yours respectfully, R.F.

A different story is recounted in Lewis Way's Memorandum[75] of his meetings with Tsar Alexander. Lewis quotes Alexander as saying, "a lady put it into my hand a paper which I put into my pocket not thinking of it at the time but afterwards I found it to be the 91st Psalm – I was much impressed with this and the words of that Psalm has been a continual support to me during the War. This is not likely to have been an anonymous "lady". Since only somebody known to the Tsar could have got that close to him the lady may well have been Barbara Krüdener and Prince Galitzin may have created the other story for the press when they all fell out.

In the early 1860s, nearly fifty years after the event, two New York State newspapers, the *Rockland County Journal*[76] and the *Geneva Courier*[77] published the same story, word for word, about Tsar Alexander I and Prince Galitzin assuming it to be true.

---

[75] *Memorandum of an interview with his Imperial Majesty Alexander Emperor of all the Russias* – 1818 -Parkes Library Special Collections, University of Southampton, MS 85 Papers of Lewis Way

[76] *The Rockland County Journal*, June 23, 1860 - *Striking Coincidence*

[77] *The Geneva Courier* December 23, 1862 - *Authentic Anecdote of Alexander I, of Russia*

Chapter 11

"Suddenly Lady Pilitzky took hold of Jacob's wrists and said, "I am not so old yet. Kiss me."
"My lady, I am not allowed to. My religion forbids it. I must humbly beg your pardon, your excellency."
"Don't apologise. I'm a fool and you're a Jew. You have borscht, not blood in your veins."
"My lady, I fear God."
"Well, go to him."

Isaac Bashevis Singer, *The Slave*

By the early nineteenth century it would have been reasonable to ask if Jesus would have recognised his own people, the Jews, or if the Jewish apostle Paul would have recognised the gentile Church he had such a hand in creating. Both had changed almost beyond recognition in nearly two thousand years, and yet both contained the memory and the seed of those heady days in Jerusalem when Jesus claimed to fulfil the Law, the Torah, once and for all in a final priestly sacrifice:

"Do not think that I have come to abolish the Law or the Prophets; I have not come to abolish them but to fulfil them."
Matthew 5:17

Many Jews believed him and followed the 'new way', many did not and waited…..and waited for Messiah to come.

By the 1800s in Europe there was much talk of other 'new ways'; the age of enlightenment, the age of reason. The French Revolution of 1789, bloody and abhorrent as it had been, had brought irreversible changes. The more or less bloodless Industrial revolution followed hard on its heels. New ideas of freedom and liberty meant the world would never be the same again, for Jew or gentile. This was the brave new world of Lewis Way and the Russian Emperor.

Many Jewish people, especially in the old German states, saw opportunities to break the mould of the ghetto mentality that had been violently imposed on them by the medieval church and many enlightened Christians saw opportunities to move forward for the mutual benefit of Jew and gentile. Both had so much to offer the modern world. There was much talk, especially at the Congress of Vienna, a conference called in 1814-15 for the winning nations to pick over the remains of Napoleon's empire and jockey for position in post-Napoleonic Europe. The Jewish emancipation movement at the conference was led by Prussian Prime Minister Prince Hardenberg[78] and Wilhelm von Humboldt[79] who saw the benefits of Jewish participation in the modern world, but reactionary forces

---

[78] Karl August von Hardenberg (1750-1822)
[79] Wilhelm von Humboldt (1767-1835) diplomat, and founder of the University of Berlin

78

at home and in other German States[80] combined to maintain the *status quo* of superstition and fear.

Conservative Jewish leaders were not blameless in holding back progress at the time either but their memories of betrayal over the centuries by Church and State were very real. The ultimate betrayal by the Nazis over a hundred years later would prove that only a Jewish State could really be trusted. In the end, little was achieved by the Congress of Vienna, but a start had been made and, in 1818, yet another conference was held, this time in Aachen, Germany, also known as Aix-La-Chapelle. The Congress of Aix-La-Chapelle was to give Lewis Way, under the patronage of the Russian Tsar, the opportunity he had sought since the day he road past *A la Ronde*. But, as his journey progressed he was learning that a reconciliation between the Church and the Jewish people who founded it would need to precede any plan for so-called 'conversion' or a mass return to the Land as new-born Christians, and reconciliation at a political and social level would need to precede even that.

Consequently Lewis would avoid any proposals that might be construed as 'conversionist'. In 1919 the Jewish journalist and lobbyist Lucien Wolf[81] would write:

At the Congress of Aix-la-Chapelle, the question was once more brought before the Great Powers. This time the initiative was taken by a well-known English conversionist, the Rev. Lewis

---

[80] Thirty-nine German states formed into the German Federation at the Congress of Vienna, 1815

[81] Lucien Wolf (1857-1930)

Way, of Stanstead (sic), Sussex. There was, however, no trace of conversionism in his efforts on this occasion, and there can be no question that the Jewish Community owe him a great debt of gratitude.[82]

The very word 'conversion' was repellent to most Jewish people anyway and carried cruel images of the forced 'conversions' to so-called Christianity in the Middle Ages and beyond, in spite of a decree by Pope Innocent III back in 1199 that "no Christian shall use violence to compel the Jews to accept baptism."[83] Jane and Mary Parminter of *A la Ronde* had themselves witnessed the supposed baptism of a Jewish woman in Rome during their travels[84] and this, far more than any tales about oak trees had moved them to take an interest in the future of the Jewish people.

But speaking to the Congress of Aix-La-Chapelle had not been part of the programme as Lewis approached Moscow and his first meeting with the Tsar. He had no plans to go any further than the Winter Palace in Saint Petersburg[85] and then back home to the wife and family he missed so much. Benjamin Nehemiah Solomon could be packed off to the Crimea, which he saw as a gateway for Jews emigrating to a renewed Israel and the job would be done. One correspondent described the Crimea as "a good jumping off place for the Holy Land."[86] However, Lewis

---

[82] *Note on the Diplomatic History of the Jewish Question*, Lucien Wolf 1919

[83] Letter on the Jews (1199), Pope Innocent III

[84] This may have been one of many forced 'baptisms' which were still not uncommon in Rome at the time and often brought great hardship to the victims.

[85] Official residence of the Russian monarchs from 1732 to 1917

[86] Letter to Alfred Rubens, 2nd February 1937

had not reckoned with the will of a truly powerful man whose title *started* with the weighty phrase, "By the Grace of God, Emperor and Autocrat of All the Russias."

Lewis would not be going home for some time.

Chapter 12

I've read the last page of the Bible. It's all going to turn out all right.

Billy Graham

On the morning of Thursday 15th January 1818, according to the Julian calendar,[87] as Lewis awaited his turn to be called to the presence of Tsar Alexander I, he was joined in his quarters in the Kremlin by a fellow supplicant, the Revd Cornelius Rahmn[88] a missionary from Sweden who was hoping to work in Siberia.

"We communed much together on the missions now sending to all parts of the world," wrote Lewis in his *Memorandum* and in particular Lewis asked him to send him reports on the fashionable theory that some of the tribes of Israel had crossed the frozen Bering land bridge from Russia to America. He asked Rahmn if, should he make it to that inhospitable land, he would:

"....bear in mind the possibility of the passage of some of the tribe of Abraham through those regions to North America as supported by William Penn, Menasseh Ben Israel and others."

---

[87] Twelve days different to the Gregorian calendar.
[88] Cornelius Rahmn (1785-1853)

Rahmn agreed to the task and they parted, having exchanged small gifts.

It seems the Emperor showed "a sympathetic interest" in Rahmn's mission and so he would set off for Irkutsk in Siberia with his pregnant wife and two year old daughter along with the English missionary Edward Stallybrass and his wife. Sadly, due to his wife's ill health, the Swede left Siberia in 1818 and, presumably, never contacted Lewis again. This interesting discussion with Reverend Rahmn was discretely interrupted by the arrival of a courtier bearing a note from Prince Alexander Gallitzin informing Lewis that "it was the pleasure of his Imperial Majesty to see me that evening at the Palace in the Kremlin at ½ past 4." The English cleric and the Russian Emperor would finally meet, and they would find themselves in such agreement on Biblical prophecy and, in particular, the future of the Jews, that Lewis would write, in Latin, to his friend William Wilberforce[89]:

"It was not an audience of a private man with an Emperor, but rather a most friendly exchange of views of a Christian with a fellow Christian. What genial condescension, what an inviting smile, what an open heart, what fiery words and what love; almost, or rather complete and absolute, divine love! It was the Spirit of God which manifested itself in this memorable interview."[90]

---

[89] *The Life of William Wilberforce*, Robert Isaac Wilberforce and Samuel Wilberforce (1838) Volume 4, p. 333

[90] *"Non erat private cujusdam cum imperatore, sed Christiani cum Christiano amicissima collation. Mores humanissimi; vultus arridens, cor apertum; loquela ardens; amor poene vel Pontius penitus divinus: talia, teste Spiritu, memorabilem hanc interlocutionem obsignaverunt."*

It wasn't until shortly after six in the evening that Lewis was finally called. "The courier came as appointed who was to conduct me to "the precise room" where I was to wait for His Imperial Majesty." They travelled by sledge within the forbidding red-brick walls of the frozen Kremlin and arrived at a private door of the new Palace. Lewis was led up a long set of stone stairs to the attic storey of the building where a door into a passage near 100 feet in length, at the end of which a servant opened yet another door. He found himself in a room with plain walls furnished with a table covered with green cloth, candles, pen and ink.

After about ten minutes, Lewis writes, "a page came in who spoke only Russian and retired without making me out." Then, in this rather Kafkaesque world, appeared an *aide-de-camp* who asked his name and, "desired me to write it, and he then wrote it upon another paper." Then another person appeared and invited Lewis to follow him through a passage and a room full of pages and attendants, who, he writes, "being accustomed, I suppose, to see nothing but staff in those upper regions, stared at a man in a black coat as a portentous phenomenon."

At last he was led through a large door which immediately closed behind him and Lewis Way found himself alone "in the presence of the first Potentate on the face of the globe." The Emperor was standing at the blazing fireplace near a large screen, dressed in an upper military coat and wearing white breeches and high black leather boots. Lewis, who claimed not to be at all nervous, bowed as soon as Alexander observed him. "He at once came forward and met me not far from the door," he records in his *Memorandum*. "He immediately took me by the hand in the most easy and condescending manner and said in English 'Mr Way I am very happy to make your acquaintance; I have heard much of you from our friends and I wish we may be known to each other.'"

There were three long tables in the room and at the corner of that nearest the fire two candles and three chairs. The Emperor invited Lewis to sit close to him, "as if he would hear best on the right side." For we were, writes Lewis a little proudly, "literally *tete-a-tete, pied-a-pied.*"

Perhaps a little pride was in order on finding himself head to head and toe to toe with the most powerful man in the world, discussing the future of the Jewish people, between one and two per-cent of the of the population of Europe in 1825, including Russia.[91] The Emperor continued modestly, "I speak English a little and understand what I read in that language but on a subject of such a nature as those on which I converse with you I cannot express myself as I wish and may sometimes use French."

"Your Majesty speaks English very correctly," said Lewis, "but I shall understand French, though not sufficiently accustomed to that language to speak it with propriety."

---

[91] Estimates vary quite widely but the European Jewish population in 1800 was 2,020,000 (including Western Europe, Eastern Europe, Balkan and former Soviet Union in Europe) according to Mark Avrum Ehrlich, *Encyclopaedia of the Jewish Diaspora: Origins, Experiences, and Culture, Volume 1* (2008). The total Population of Europe, including Russia in 1800 was 187,000,000 according to R. Cameron, *A Concise Economic History of the World* (1993). Therefore 1.08% in 1800 and rising by 1825

His Majesty then continued in English, which he enjoyed and spoke rather well. Alan Palmer in his biography of Alexander says that as a child "he was remarkably slow in picking up the French language."[92] But it was the language of the court, and the preferred language of his influential grandmother, so he had persevered. Russian was not an option for the nobility.

The Tsar continued in English and Lewis listened attentively. "The object of your journey is very interesting and one in which I feel much concern. You may be assured I will do all that lies in my power to assist in it. I consider your coming to Russia on this occasion as a providential concurrence of circumstances - each must do his part, and in time, by the blessing of God, something may be done. My office is a very laborious one and requires the chief part of my time, but my great source of pleasure is to read the Scriptures and think on these things."
This was all that Lewis could have hoped for, and he made his move.

"Your Majesty's disposition is well known to us in England. When I had the honour to see your Majesty on board the vessel[93] at Portsmouth[94] I much wished to have had an opportunity of saying a few words on behalf of the

---

[92] Alan Palmer, *Alexander I Tsar of War and Peace* , 1974
[93] Duke of Clarence's flagship the *Impregnable*
[94] The Allied sovereigns' visit to England occurred in June 1814 to celebrate the peace following the defeat of France and abdication of Napoleon Bonaparte in April 1814. The sovereigns and generals of the Coalition Allies - comprising Austria, Prussia, Russia, Sweden, the United Kingdom, and a number of German States – took part in a state visit and various peace celebrations in London before progressing to the Congress of Vienna later that year.

Jews but I am glad that occasion was denied me as the part your Majesty has since taken in the cause shows most clearly that the Society in England and that in Russia have been acting independently of each other and the same good Providence will conduct the operations of the two bodies to the same destination. I believe your Majesty to be influenced by the grace of God and I have often prayed that your Majesty may receive the help promised in Scripture to those who help the children of Abraham."

"When persons give themselves up to the service of God," replied the Tsar, "they will be taught their path of duty and enabled to follow it by divine grace and teaching. I have read the Bible attentively and made it the rule of my conduct however impossibly since 1815 and before and found it furnished me with support in long times of need." At this he rose and brought his four volume Louis Segond[95] French translation of the Bible to the table where they sat together and he touchingly explained that he had missed out on Bible teaching in his school days. "My religious education was neglected by the Empress Catherine who chiefly superintended, and attended to politics more than religion."

He showed Lewis how he now read the Bible. A chapter in the Old Testament, a chapter in the Gospel and a chapter in the Epistles every day, which he noted on a card neatly divided in compartments. He had now read the Bible four times in succession marking with a pencil those parts he understood. "I found", said the Emperor, "I could not understand many parts of the New Testament without the

---

[95] Louis Segond (1810–1885), was a Swiss theologian who translated the Bible into French from the original Hebrew and Greek.

Old. I have always found the New Testament to be a key to the Old and the Old the real commentary on the New."

Alexander now seems to have warmed to his guest and began to open his heart to the sincere Anglican clergyman who had come so far in faith. For a short while their mutual faith would transcend the barriers of class and language. At one point, conscious of the friendship which was developing, Lewis Way said, "Your Majesty must suppose I feel some difficulty in speaking on subjects of such delicacy and importance in your Majesty's presence." The Emperor replied, "You ought to have none. Whatever the relative position of Christians in this life may be, they are all brethren; and when only two are gathered in the presence of God in their hearts they know and understand each other."

The Emperor then read from his French Bible and from then on spoke French as if only being able to really express theological ideas clearly in that language. Lewis more or less kept up but had to admit to struggling sometimes with the barrage of unfamiliar French. At one point he confesses, "His Majesty here made some remarks with great animation which I do not write because I cannot distinctly recollect them, but they led at last to the care of the Jews I there found." Whatever political reality might come to pass and whatever changes might be forced upon him in the future, in 1818 Alexander sincerely cared for the Jews of Russia and had a heart for Israel.

And so, as Lewis's loyal daughter Drusilla would write many years later:

It was [Alexander's] express wish that my father meet him at the Congress in Aix-la-Chapelle, in order to lay before the gathering of notables there and bring close to their hearts, the matter of the Jews."

Chapter 13

In a profound sense every man has two halves to his being; he is not one person so much as two persons trying to act in unison. I believe that in the heart of each human being there is something which I can only describe as a "child of darkness" who is equal and complementary to the more obvious "child of light."

Laurens Van der Post, *Journey into Russia, 1964*

The Congress of Aix-la-Chapelle was not due to start until October 1818, nine months away so Alexander thought Lewis should accompany Benjamin Nehemiah Solomon, his companion on the trip from England, to the Crimea to begin the work among the Karaites (Karaim), who, he claimed, were eager for information about Christianity. There was no argument - his friend had spoken, and his friend was, after all, Emperor of all the Russias! Alexander would meet him in Crimea on the Black Sea.

The Karaites were Jews who did not accept the authority of any book but the Jewish Bible, the *Tanakh*, or the Old Testament. Karaite Judaism rejected the principal that the Rabbis were the sole authorities for interpreting the Bible and they rejected the Rabbinic Oral Law found in the Talmud and Mishnah. Their Biblical authority, they claimed, was Deuteronomy 4:2:

"Do not add to what I command you and do not subtract from it, but keep the commands of the Lord your God that I give you."

They would learn to understand the Bible truths through personal study and prayer. They took a pragmatic approach to the Law (*Torah*). Such a view clearly appealed to the English Evangelicals who no doubt saw a parallel with their own view of Roman Catholicism at the time which, they believed, did not encourage individuals to read the Bible, Old or New Testament, but to depend on the teaching authority of the Church, the *Magisterium*, delivered through the Bishops and the parish priests.[96]

For this reason, among others, the London Society had sent Benjamin Nehemiah Solomon, at Lewis's expense, to evangelise the Jewish Karaites of Crimea. Like the Tsar they also saw it as a convenient gateway to the Holy Land for those who wished to return. Lewis himself saw it primarily as a cover for his own programme with the Tsar, to improve the lot of Jews in the Russian Empire and elsewhere. But he hadn't expected to do all the work himself. Within three months Lewis and Benjamin Solomon would be on the Smolensk road to Odessa on the Black Sea 706 miles south of Moscow, via Minsk and Kiev where they met many Jewish communities. It was in the

---

[96] The downside of such freedom, so far as the Church was concerned, both Catholic and Protestant, was that within Lewis Way's lifetime organisations such as the Mormons, the Church of Jesus Christ of Latter-day Saints, were teaching an understanding of the Bible which denied the fundamental beliefs of the Christian Church. This included a radically different teaching of the Trinity, the Incarnation and the Resurrection which was drawing people away from the mainline churches.

seaport of Odessa that Lewis learnt he was the father of a baby daughter who by then was already two months old, and had been christened Catherine Louisa,[97] after his friend Princess Louise of Posen.

Lewis would meet the Emperor in the Crimean capital, Simferopol, on Saturday 18th May 1818. The ancient city was relatively warm after the long cold winter of the north but the team would not be there long enough to experience the Black Sea resort sunshine that would be favoured by senior Communist Party apparatchiks in later years. Lewis was initially taken to the Governor's house where the courtyard was:

"illuminated with lights on the ground and rails in the Russian style to an anti-room delightfully perfumed by lemon and citron trees in full fruit."

After much formality Lewis was driven to Government House. More formality followed as officers and servants led him slowly to the Emperor's private room. Lewis takes up the story:

"His Majesty met me at the door and took my hand just as he had done at Moscow, and addressed me in English - 'Sit down here, and tell me where you have been, and what you have seen!'"

Lewis continues with barely concealed awe:

---

[97] Catherine Louisa 1818-1906

"Hearing that I was speaking a little hoarse his physician gave me a few drops that cured me immediately. I then ran over my journey from Moscow to Minsk and mentioned the circumstances of that place and others. I submitted the practice of the Polish Jews refusing early marriages."[98]

The two friends sat down, close together, "his Majesty being deaf," and read together chapter thirteen of the Gospel of Mark in which Jesus, seated on the Mount of Olives and looking across the Kidron Valley to the Temple in Jerusalem, told his disciples what the future would be like. They must not be deceived; they must be on their guard. Many would come claiming to be the Jewish Messiah. "Everyone will hate you because of me, but the one who stands firm to the end will be saved." (Mark 13:13).

Having read together Lewis produced a paper entitled *Signs of the Last Days* and the Emperor apparently read it avidly. In his *Memorandum* Lewis reports a conversation with the Tsar on the 'New Jerusalem' featured in the last chapter of the New Testament which, Lewis said:

"....may signify the happy state of the church after conversion of the Jews as compared with the prophets. Your Majesty observes a new earth cannot be in heaven, the city is represented as coming down not going up. It refers to the glorious church below. The exact day is only known to God. The Lord gives his disciples a

---

[98] *Memorandum of an interview with his Imperial Majesty Alexander Emperor of all the Russias – 1818* - Parkes Library Special Collections, University of Southampton, MS 85 Papers of Lewis Way

sign the time is near. Great tribulation and earthquake, the destruction of the Anti-Christ and all who opposes religion."

At the end of a long and intense evening which took them past midnight, the Tsar announced his plans for his friend. Lewis would attend the international conference at Aix-la-Chapelle and present the case for Jewish rights and emancipation to the great powers represented there. And in the time honoured way of such friendships between powerful rulers and their less powerful friends, there was no debate, no options. This was another heavy blow to Lewis's tender heart; there was now no chance of vising England before the conference in the summer for even a brief sight of his new daughter. He would have to stay in the Crimea to set up the mission with Benjamin Nehemiah Solomon and then move more or less directly to Aix-la-Chapelle, leaving Solomon in charge.

It may be that the perceptive Alexander did not entirely trust Solomon to see the job through, and this view was apparently born out when, after some years, he is supposed to have absconded with £300 of the London Society's funds and was, according to historian Anna Marie Stirling, never seen again, [99]which was not entirely true. She also claims Joseph Wolff[100] told Lewis Way that he did not trust Solomon and quotes Wolff's words to British banker Henry Drummond Jr assuming they were spoken to Lewis Way, "That man [Solomon] is not sincere, he will break out terribly some day![101]"

---

[99] *The Ways of Yesterday*, A.M.W. Stirling, 1930
[100] Joseph Wolff (1795-1862)
[101] *Travels and Adventures of the Rev. Joseph Wolff*, Joseph Wolff, 1861

That occasion may have been when in 1821 Solomon returned to England and visited Lewis to discuss some theological issues concerning the Trinity which had been bothering him. Lewis arranged for him to see the Biblical commentator Revd Thomas Scott[102] who seems, over a period of three months, to have got Solomon through what may have been a crisis of faith or a natural enquiry for any intelligent monotheistic Jew. Solomon had planned to accompany Alexander McCaul, an English missionary and author, to Warsaw, but wrote from Amsterdam to Algernon Sydney Thelwall an evangelical Church of England clergyman that the condition of his wife and children in Galicia (today in the Ukraine) obliged him to return home. Aaron Bernstein, author of *Some Jewish Witnesses for Christ* reports that "[Solomon's] own father declared to the missionary Smith, in 1827, that he was living as a Christian."

Also, in his *Missionary Journal Volume III* published in 1829 in an entry dated 2 July 1825 the respected Wolff had written, contrary to what he would say at the end of his life in 1862:

I met at Teflis a Jew, Lorwiez, by name, who was convinced of the truth of Christianity by Benjamin Nehemiah Solomon, the late Missionary of the London Society, when at Odessa. I must here observe, to the honour of my nation, that I know the reason of Mr Solomon's determination to leave suddenly the Society, and I have strong reasons for believing that Mr Solomon has done it from good motives; if I had been in his situation, I would perhaps have done the same. It is believed, that Solomon is in

---

[102] Revd Thomas Scott (1747-1821)

Moldavia.[103] *I have likewise strong reasons to believe that he has remained faithful to his Saviour.*

If the Emperor had any doubts about Solomon's management skills he did not seem to doubt his missionary commitment. From the beginning he had placed such confidence in Solomon that he issued, through Prince Galitzin, the following authority:

CERTIFICATE

The bearer of these presents, Benjamin Nehemiah Solomon, a Hebrew by descent, having embraced the Christian religion in England, and subsequently admitted into Ecclesiastical Orders, at present sojourning in Russia by Imperial permission, is intrusted to me by his Imperial Majesty, to procure for him special protection in every place of his residence. Wherefore all local authorities, Ecclesiastical and Secular, are to afford to the said B.N. Solomon, as a preacher of the Word of God among the Hebrews, every protection, defence, and all possible assistance, so that in case of necessity, he may receive from the authorities in all places due co-operation and safeguard, in the free exercise of his official duty, without any impediment whatsoever.

In witness whereof is this instrument granted, with my signature and the arms of my seal affixed thereto.

The Minister of Religion and National Civilization. Prince Alex. Galitzin[104].
Moscow, 20th Feb., 1818.[105]

---

[103] Today the Republic of Moldova
[104] Prince Alexander Galitzin was also president of the Russian Bible Society at this time.
[105] W.T. Gidney, *The History of the London Society for Promoting Christianity Amongst the Jews from 1809 to 1908*, 1908, p. 95

Sadly, by 1820 the Tsar's concern for the future prospects of the Jewish people began to wane, which probably accounts for Benjamin's departure for England.

The *Jewish Encyclopaedia* of 1909 tells us that:

After the Congress [of Aix-la-Chapelle] Alexander altogether abandoned his former liberal ideas and adopted a reactionary policy. Owing to this, the following restrictive measures characterized the closing years of the czar's reign: The rescript of May 4, 1820, forbidding Jews to keep Christian servants; that of Aug. 10, 1824, prohibiting foreign Jews from settling permanently in Russia; and the edict of Jan. 13, 1825, removing the Jews from villages to towns and cities in the governments of Mohilev and Vitebsk.

There is no record of where or when the Revd Benjamin Nehemiah Solomon died and perhaps it is not a biographer's job to speculate, but it would be nice to think that he returned to his wife Sarah, and the children, and settled down as an Anglican clergyman, somewhere in Galicia.

Chapter 14

Sometimes the dreams that come true are the dreams you never even knew you had."

Alice Sebold, *The Lovely Bones*

Having settled Benjamin Nehemiah Solomon in the Crimea Lewis left Russia by way of Brody (in present day Ukraine) entering the Austrian Empire on 1st July 1818, travelling in relative comfort on the modern, well maintained turnpike roads of the western world. With him was his trusty secretary Maberley, the Revd Cox having been sent home for not speaking French, Sultan Kategerry-Krhimgerry the Tartar nobleman having stayed in Russia and Benjamin Nehemiah Solomon having been left with the Karaites in the Crimea.

According to Joseph Wolff, Sultan Kategerry-Krhimgerry, a Muslim by birth, had been sent by Tsar Alexandra I to study in Edinburgh, where he got baptised, joined the Church of Scotland and married a Miss Nielson.[106] How he joined up with Lewis Way is not clear. Lewis and Maberley seem to have travelled by *chaise* to Prague and Vienna but would later pick up the original carriage from Berlin via Potsdam on the great circular route from Brussels to Aix-la-Chapelle.

---

[106] *Travels and Adventures of the Rev. Joseph Wolff*, Joseph Wolff, 1861

It was in Prague, now capital of the Czech Republic, in the summer of 1818 that Lewis would visit the Jewish cemetery and seems to have discovered a deep and mystical relationship with the Jewish people which previously had been one of mere prophetic expediency *i.e.* the Jews must return to the Land before the Messiah can return so let's help to get that under way. The missing element seems to have been love, and subsequently it was said of Lewis, according to family historian A.M.W. Stirling in 1930, that he was the first Christian to convince the Jews that it was possible for a Christian to love them![107] Perhaps he was not the first but after centuries of hatred from the world it was a timely epiphany for one who would influence kings and emperors in spite of his own doubts and fears. He explains:

"The Jews' burial ground is the most extraordinary place I ever visited. In it are not to say a great many graves because nothing short of millions can convey any idea of what there must be collected in that spot of Death and decay and Earthly Oblivion.......... I cannot describe, for I could not analyse, the singular sensations and ideas which thronged my mind as I rather crept than walked about its tortuous and gloomy paths. It has long been disused from necessity. Far in, under the old elders, and all but inaccessible, can be seen among the crowd of tombstones fragments of costly monuments, green with moss and the mouldy lichens of centuries. Think of the wealth and secret splendour, the misery and persecution, the bearded dignity

---

[107] "Subsequently it was said of Lewis Way that he was the first Christian to convince the Jews that it was possible for a Christian to love them!" *The Ways of Yesterday*, A.M.W. Stirling, 1930, p. 136

and black-eyed beauty that have come through that narrow gate to rest in oblivion!

There is something to me affecting in this place, the extraordinary story of this people as a nation, their sufferings and persecutions and tortures in the darker ages, their dispersion as individuals and unity as a people were all suggested at the locale. And this crowding together as it were for refuge after death from a world which held them in abhorrence, struck me as peculiarly melancholy and touching."

The old cemetery was still in use until 1787 but today it lies alongside the 20th century Jewish Museum, a silent witness to many more Jewish deaths that were to come, a bus ride away at the old Theresienstadt ghetto.[108]

"During the peak of Theresienstadt's overcrowding in 1944, some 59,000 Jews were packed into a 750-square-metre area."[109] Most were transported to death camps, to be murdered, more Jewish blood on the long road to Armageddon.

Prague had been a 114 mile detour north from Lewis's route through Brody to Vienna. We cannot tell if he was sent or called there but he was certainly changed on his return from this Damascene diversion. Lewis would never lose his millennial zeal, but from now on the documents he would prepare for the Congress would be, as Nathan Feinberg writes,

---

[108] Terezin to the Czechs
[109] *The Yad Vashem Encyclopaedia of the Ghettos During the Holocaust*, Yad Vashem 2009

"composed in earnest sympathy and admiration for the Jewish people."[110]

Lewis and his small entourage moved on from Prague to Vienna, following the scenic route to Aix-la-Chapelle, taking in Bern, Lausanne, Geneva, Dijon, Fontainebleau, Paris and Brussels. From there, completing a great circular route, to Magdeburg, Brandenburg, Potsdam, Frankfurt-am-Main, Mainz, Coblenz, Cologne and, finally, arriving in Aix-la-Chapelle on 24th October 1818. It is unlikely he would have the opportunity to visit most of these places again in his lifetime, besides which he had promised the faithful Maberley a visit to Chamonix, host village of Mont Blanc, the highest mountain in the Alps. As they finally approached Aix-la-Chapelle Lewis began to realise the scale not only of his task but the event itself.

Thousands of visitors filled the cobbled streets, damp with early autumn mist. From entertainers and artists to confidence tricksters and pickpockets, food sellers to soothsayers, everybody trying to make a living, one way or another. For those with a taste for culture there was an exhibition of paintings at the historic *Rathaus* (City Hall) featuring works by Sir Thomas Lawrence (1769-1830) Karl Begas, the German historical painter born at Heinsberg near Aix-la-Chapelle (1794-1854) and Friedrich Wilhelm Ternite (1786-1871). While he was there Lawrence would paint what he called, 'the three greatest monarchs in recent political importance', as well as Hardenberg, Richelieu, Castlereagh and "Old Nosey", the Duke of Wellington.

---

[110] *The Jewish Question at the Congress of Aix-la-Chapelle, 1818*, Nathan Feinberg

And the 'heroic' German actor Ferdinand Esslair was in town playing Karl Moor, hero of Schiller's *Die Räuber* and the mediaeval German hero Wallenstein, as well as the more familiar William Tell and Othello.

Accommodation was all booked up, everything was overpriced. Everybody was making the most of the six week Congress, from waiters to the high-class prostitutes the ancient city had acquired a reputation for in the 19th century. The blue, white and gold of the Royal Prussian Army brightened the autumn days as they clattered around the ancient town. Several battalions had arrived on 13th September ahead of the Congress along with a squadron of Hussars to keep order and represent the power of the host, King Friedrich Wilhelm III of Prussia. Some soldiers stayed in the 1660 Carmelite convent which had been dissolved by the French in 1802, others in pubs, some in the refurbished barracks.

Even for a city that entertained fifty thousand pilgrims at a time resources were at a premium. Aachen, as the German city is known today, was, and is, one of the most important venues for Christian pilgrimage, together with Jerusalem, Rome and Santiago de Compostela. This ancient Rhineland spa town is the old capital of the Holy Roman Empire and the Cathedral, a UNESCO World Cultural Heritage site, contains the mortal remains of the Emperor Charlemagne[111]in a shining gold and silver casket dating from 1215. In the Emperor's original octagonal Palatine Chapel is suspended the magnificent Barbarossa

---

[111] Charlemagne aka Charles the Great (742-814).

Chandelier representing the New Jerusalem of Revelation 21 which would surely have appealed to Lewis:

I saw the Holy City, the new Jerusalem, coming down out of heaven from God, prepared as a bride beautifully dressed for her husband. Revelation 21:2

Fifty miles west-southwest of Cologne, Aachen borders the wide flat countryside of the Netherlands and Belgium, leading to the sea and the land immortalised in Jacques Brel's song *Le Plat Pays*. In Lewis Way's time it bordered just the Netherlands as the state of Belgium would not be created until 1830. Before that it bordered France. When Napoleon's France was defeated Europe had been cut up in 1815 at the Congress of Vienna by Britain, Russia, Prussia, and Austria. It just remained for the Congress of Aix-la-Chapelle in 1818 to tidy up the details, settle the accounts with Royalist France and make plans for peace and prosperity in post-Napoleonic Europe.

Just seven powerful men, plenipotentiaries, would make the final decisions on behalf of their rulers, an absent ruler in the case of the Duke of Wellington as the Hanoverian George III stayed at home. The other six were Robert Stewart, Viscount Castlereagh, for Great Britain, Klemens von Metternich for Austria, Karl August von Hardenberg and Christian Gunther Bernstorff for Prussia. Russia was represented by Count Karl Robert Nesselrode and Capodistrias. The Duke of Richelieu had a courtesy place on behalf of occupied France. In addition to these major players, according to documents in the City Archives, there were the following:

2 Kaiser (Emperors)
1 Kaiserin (Empress)
1 König (King)
2 Kronprinzen (Crown Princes)
2 Großfürsten (Grand Dukes)
3 Herzöge (Dukes)
1 Herzogin (Duchess)
13 Fürsten (heads of princely houses of German origin e.g. Liechtenstein today)
1 Fürstin (female of above)
7 Prinzen (Princes)
1 Prinzessin (Princess)
37 Grafen (Counts)
8 Gräfinnen (Countesses)
1 Staatskanzler (Chancellor)
15 Staatsminister (Minister of State)
43 Generale (Generals)
I Admiral (Admiral)

Not to mention……

18 Bankiers (Bankers) including Rothschild, Bethmann and Baring.
24 Musiker (Musicians)
17 Maler (Artists)

And to this galaxy of European royalty and worthies Lewis Way, a humble lawyer and Anglican clergyman would speak, just two days before the end of the Congress, and would be listened to. Tsar Alexander had arrived in Aix-la-Chapelle on 28th September 1818, along with Kaiser Franz I of Austria. He would meet with Lewis on 11th October and again, finally, on 15th November 1818. Lewis had sent the Tsar a number of memoranda[112] on the "Jewish Question" which he would submit to the plenipotentiaries.

---

[112] They were later published in Paris as *"Mémoires sur l'Etat des Israélites Dédiés et Présentés à Leurs Majestés Impériales et Royales, Réunies au Congrès d' Aix-la-Chapelle"*

The first session would be attended by Alexander, the Emperor Francis I of Austria, and Frederick William III of Prussia. The meetings would take place in the residences of Count Hardenberg at *Bettendorfsches Haus am Markt,* today the pleasant Café Extrablatt, and Metternich's quarters at Karlsbad, *Komphausbadstrasse,* which is now a brunch bar called Alex. Both of these sites are within easy walking distance of the *Rathaus* and the Hanwurst sausage restaurant where Lewis and the Tsar might have met for the last time to enjoy Bratwurst and beer together, if only the franchise had existed in 1818.

Chapter 15

They took over from the old order not only most of its customs, conventions, and modes of thought, but even those ideas which prompted our revolutionaries to destroy it; that, in fact, though nothing was further from their intentions, they used the debris of the old order for building up the new.

Alexis de Tocqueville, *The Old Regime and the French Revolution*

From 1815, after Napoleon had offered the Jews equality within his empire and beyond, the Jewish people hadn't counted for much in the great scheme of things and much less towards the end of this "new age" of science, even though they would play a major, and disproportionate part in its development. Napoleon, who many saw as the so-called Biblical 'Antichrist' although he had been a good friend to the Jews, had been defeated, and now reactionary forces were gathering in Aix-la-Chapelle. The future looked bright for the *Ancien Régime* in a united Europe, but not for the Jews, who stood to lose almost everything they had gained under the influence of Napoleon and the Revolution of 1789.

Lewis was no revolutionary but he had become a man with a mission after his time with the charismatic Russian Emperor. He had an opportunity to speak to some of the most powerful and influential people in the world at that time. James Monroe was fifth President of the United States, the last president who had been a Founding Father, but America had not yet made its debut on the world stage, Europe was still the centre of world power and they all came together at Aix-la-Chapelle, the centre of their world, for forty-six days.[113] And on the forty-sixth day they would sign a document that would bridge the thousand year old gap between Jew and Christian. Not everybody may have been ready to cross the bridge but Lewis Way had built it and it remains to this day.

With the support of the Tsar of Russia he made this plea:

1. All civil and social rights should be accorded to the Israelites without any difference from those enjoyed by the Christians.

2. The governments should induce their priests, and especially the bishops, to preach to their fullest ability both by their example and their speech the widest charity toward the children of Israel.

3 The governments should encourage the establishment of arts and trades among the Israelites and, above all, to direct them toward agriculture, to reward those who make progress and to take into their employ those who are capable of usefully filling positions.

---

[113] 1st October to 15th November 1818

4   The governments should make regulations to enable the Jewish youth to participate in general education to the same extent as the Christians, in the same colleges, gymnasiums, universities etc.

5   To accomplish a project so conducive to the well-being of the Israelites it is necessary to establish a central committee composed of enlightened Christian and Jewish members at Frankfort, at Berlin and Warsaw, or in some other place.

The objects with which this committee would occupy itself would be:

1.   To establish general correspondence regarding the Israelites in all parts of the world.

2.   To encourage the publication of such works as will aim to put an end to prejudice, to uproot hatred, and to maintain a mutual spirit of good-will and harmony.

3.   To examine different writings opposing the admission of Israelites to civil rights which may appear, and to refute them.

4.   Finally, this committee would undertake to ascertain the best means of reforming and perfecting the civil, moral and religious state of the children of Israel, to spread and promote mutual education among them and the taste for the mechanical and liberal arts.

It had started at Vienna but Lewis would close the deal at Aix-la-Chapelle. The plenipotentiaries listened and declared:

"Without entering into the merits of the views entertained by the author of the project [Lewis Way], the Conference recognises the justice of his general tendency, and takes cognisance of the fact that the plenipotentiaries of Austria and Prussia [Metternich and Hardenberg] have declared themselves ready to furnish all possible information concerning the Jewish situation in those monarchies, in order to clarify a problem which must claim the attention equally of the statesman and the humanitarian."

It was signed by Metternich for Austria, Hardenberg and Barnstorff, for Prussia, Richelieu for France, Castlereagh and Wellington for Britain, Nesselrode and Capodistrias for Russia. The document they signed was not legally binding, it made no great commitments but it recognised the Jewish people as fellow travellers in the world, crossing and re-crossing the bridge Lewis had built at Aix-la-Chapelle.

Way's achievement should not be underestimated. Like the Balfour Declaration[114] ninety-nine years later it would

---

[114] Foreign Office, November 2nd, 1917 Dear Lord Rothschild,
I have much pleasure in conveying to you on behalf of His Majesty's government, the following declaration of sympathy with Jewish Zionist aspirations which has been submitted to, and approved, by the Cabinet:
His Majesty's Government view with favour the establishment in Palestine of a national home for the Jewish people, and will use their best endeavours to facilitate the achievement of this object, it being clearly understood that nothing shall be done which may prejudice the civil and religious rights of existing non-Jewish communities in

be "more honour'd in the breach than the observance"[115] but as Max J. Kohler writes in his introduction to *Jewish Rights at the Congress of Vienna (1814-1815), and Aix-la-Chapelle (1818)*:

"Probably for the first time in modern history, Jewish emancipation was officially passed upon at a conference of nations, and a resolution in favour of the principle [of Jewish rights] was adopted......"

Professor Nathan Feinberg observes in his paper *The Jewish Question at the Congress of Aix-la-Chapelle, 1818,*[116] that Lewis Way "was not the only petitioner at Aix-la-Chapelle." Petitions were heard on behalf of the anti-slavery movement (Thomas Clarkson), the working classes (Robert Owen) as well as several Jewish groups seeking civil rights. Even Napoleon's mother, Letizia Ramolino, petitioned the Congress for the release of her son from St Helena, but this, not surprisingly, was dismissed.

Only Lewis Way's petition "won the attention of the Congress" and resulted in an historic decision.

Palestine, or the rights and political status enjoyed by Jews in any other country.
I should be grateful if you would bring this declaration to the knowledge of the Zionist Federation.
Yours, Arthur James Balfour
[115] Shakespeare, *Hamlet*
[116] *Israel Yearbook on Human Rights* (1972)

Chapter 16

I had a dream, which was not all a dream.
The bright sun was extinguish'd, and the stars
Did wander darkling in the eternal space,
Rayless, and pathless, and the icy earth
Swung blind and blackening in the moonless air;
Morn came and went - and came, and brought no day,
And men forgot their passions in the dread
Of this their desolation; and all hearts
Were chill'd into a selfish prayer for light:

Lord Byron, *Darkness*

In the summer of 2013 I sat with my wife in the air-conditioned comfort of the appropriately named *Alex* brunch bar in Aachen, the present day, German name for Aix-la-Chapelle. *Caffè latte* in hand, we stared across the *Komphausbadstrasse* where, two hundred years before, Lewis Way would have stood outside the temporary home of Metternich and prepared to leave Aix-la-Chapelle for England. The last meeting of the Congress was over and *Karlsbad*, the Austrian plenipotentiary's temporary home, would have a new tenant. In the warm afternoon sun the bright menu cover offered tempting ice cold lemon tea as one of its *'Sommer Drinks'*. The red and white bendy buses passed by with the clockwork precision of German toys and we looked across two blocks in the direction of the new synagogue at 23 *Synagogenplatz*. Rebuilt by the people of Aachen in 1995 its great glass frontage seemed to defy the mindless window breaking destruction of *Kristallnacht* in 1938 that destroyed the old one.

For a moment the modern city disappeared. The Revd Lewis Way adjusted his bicorn hat, *de rigueur* in spite of the summer sun, and headed for his quarters. There was still much work to do. But the party was over, the fair was leaving town, and he had a result. Alone now, amid the doubts that always follow success, especially if that success displeases the devil, Lewis began to question himself.

Yes, it may be true that he said, "Such an appeal has not been made for the poor Jews since the days of Mordecai and Esther!" but if he did it was just a sound bite. Lewis was a poet, a contemporary and admirer of the flamboyant Byron. He even wrote a sonnet on Byron's death and published it as an appendix to his own major work, *Palingenesia – The World to Come*. That's how he saw it. He had come before the kings on behalf of the Jews of Europe, and won the day. Queen Esther would have been proud of him.

Like Esther, he knew well enough the source of power that made this impossible hour possible and he knew how easily it could be lost. Within a year Alexander would backpedal and would not support Lewis's attempt to raise the Jewish question at future Congresses. Within a year most of the German states had reverted to their medieval ways. Perhaps only Britain and the emerging United States had a real diaspora home for the Chosen People. But he would preach and he would travel. The bridge had been built, but it would be for others to cross. Shortly before

Christmas 1818 Lewis Way returned to England. The five surviving children would celebrate Christmas with their father, and Mary and Lewis would celebrate their seventeenth wedding anniversary on the last day of the year. They hadn't seen each other for a year and four months, and Lewis had never seen his baby daughter Catherine Louisa.

The new year would see the first glimmering rays of a dawning new era, the age of steam power and the coming Victorian age. The future Queen Victoria would be born on 24th May 1819 and the *SS Savannah*, a hybrid steam and sailing ship, became the first steamship to cross the Atlantic Ocean, arriving at Liverpool from Savannah, Georgia on 20th June 1819. Steel and steam would move the world on towards Armageddon in ways Lewis could not have imagined. Lewis Way, like many of his fellow Evangelicals trusted the Bible to give them a glimpse of the future, but only a glimpse. Jesus *would* return to judge the world, the Jewish people *would* return to the Land, but not before they would be nearly wiped out by an antichrist committed to their total annihilation, Adolph Hitler.

Lewis would never lose his enthusiasm for 'end times prophecy' or his commitment to the future of God's dispersed people, the Jews. But as history moved on he might have remembered the cautionary words of the Apostle Paul, "For we know in part, and we prophesy in part" (1 Corinthians 13:9). A glimmer of light had shone through the dark shadow of anti-Semitism and Lewis Way's achievement at Aix-la-Chapelle should not be undervalued, but we are reminded by St Paul, continuing at verse 12 of 1 Corinthians, "For now we see through a glass, darkly, but then face to face: now I know in part; but then shall I know even as also I am known."

Chapter 17

It was all very well for an Englishman like Mr Fogg to make the tour of the world with a carpet-bag; a lady could not be expected to travel comfortably under such conditions.

Jules Verne, *Around the World in 80 Days* (1873)

It had been a long warm summer in the England of 1818, the warmest in living memory, some said. Cricket was slowly recovering from the effects of the Napoleonic wars and high fashion was returning from its natural home in Paris to the streets of London. But for the Way children, especially Drusilla and Albert, now teenagers, it had been their second summer without a father's presence and influence. Perhaps as a result Drusilla would remain very close to her father and would defend his memory publicly in the cynical world of the late nineteenth century. She lived into her eighties and never married.

Albert, the only surviving son, known to the family as 'Atty' would take to the law, like Lewis, but after his father's death he would pursue his preferred career as an antiquarian. Baby Catherine Louisa would live through the Victorian age and see many changes in her world including the first Zionist Congress of 1897. She outlived Queen Victoria by five years. The younger girls Anna Mary Charlotte Eliza and Olivia both married well as would Georgiana Millicent, their last child, who would be born in 1820.

Whatever the effects of over a year's absence the five surviving children would soon be taken on the journey of a lifetime, more or less together, as compensation. This 'grand tour' would be partly for their education but it also gave Lewis an opportunity to rent out the Stansted estate for a couple of years to take the pressure off his diminishing fortune. The so called Grand Tour was originally intended as the culmination of an upper class young man's education in the 18th century and would take him, along with a retinue of servants and guides, to the cultural centres of Florence, Rome and Naples by way of the Pont du Gard, Nice and the Côte d'Azur. Prior to the coming of the railway this was the standard route and it did not include Greece. Most young upper class girls could usually only look forward to 'coming out' in society with a view to marriage but there were, of course, notable exceptions, one of which was the notorious Lady Hester Stanhope, of whom more later.

Drusilla Way herself was not cut out for the social marriage machine and would make her way in life independently with the aid of a considerable inheritance from her mother's uncle.

Lewis planned to extend the basic Italian tour package as far as Jerusalem for himself and Albert. Drusilla would gladly have joined them, and greatly wished to, but while the two men could easily find accommodation in the various monasteries along the way, ladies were not welcomed as guests at that time. Meanwhile, Lewis had commitments arising from the work in Russia, the future of the College needed to be dealt with and Albert would finish his secondary education. He was educated at home, acquiring, along with other subjects, a knowledge of most European languages as well as Hebrew and Old English. On his return from the tour in 1824 he would matriculate at Trinity College, Cambridge and eventually graduate in 1829.

In the autumn of 1822 the Stansted estate would be leased for two years to London businessman John Julius Angerstein[117] to whom Lewis had a family connection through a niece of his grandfather, also Lewis Way. The wealthy Angerstein, founder of the National Gallery in London, had apparently shown an interest in the property and would, according to a draft contract dated 1818, pay £2,000 a year in quarterly instalments:

"....to be made at Christmas, Easter, Midsummer and Michaelmas."

In addition he would be permitted:

"....the usual quantity of deer during the term of his tenancy the same never exceeding 25 bucks and 20 does within the year."

---

[117] John Julius Angerstein (1735-1823)

Chapter 18

England 1819

An old, mad, blind, despised, and dying King;
Princes, the dregs of their dull race, who flow
Through public scorn, - mud from a muddy spring;
Rulers who neither see nor feel nor know,
But leechlike to their fainting country cling
Till they drop, blind in blood, without a blow.
A people starved and stabbed in th' untilled field;
An army, whom liberticide and prey
Makes as a two-edged sword to all who wield;
Golden and sanguine laws which tempt and slay;
Religion Christless, Godless - a book sealed;
A senate, Time's worst statute, unrepealed -
Are graves from which a glorious Phantom may
Burst, to illumine our tempestuous day.

Percy Bysshe Shelley, *England in 1819*

While the revolutionary and atheistic poet Shelley awaited his apocalyptic "glorious Phantom" the world of Lewis Way in 1819 reflected a gentler, more hopeful world, though not without its own Apocalypse in the coming judgement of the resurrected Jesus.

But beyond the security of Stansted the introduction of the Corn Laws, the general poverty following the Napoleonic

Wars and the reaction by the landed classes against any kind of reform would culminate that year in the so-called Peterloo Massacre. A group of some seventy thousand demonstrating reformers in St Peter's Field, Manchester were attacked by cavalry under orders from the local magistrates. Fifteen people died, four to five hundred were injured. Revolution was still an option in England.

Meanwhile, in faraway rural Sussex, Stansted had become the fashionable place to be invited to, and to be seen. The delightful children, Lewis's charming wife and even the estate staff and villagers, not necessarily *"a people starved and stabbed in th' untilled field,"* according to Shelley, made Stansted a spiritual bolthole for the intellectual elite of Georgian London. The endless grounds and parkland kept the wider world at bay and great minds could dream dreams and prepare for challenges, real and imagined, to come. Among the regular A-list guests, or what daughter Drusilla called "number one guests" was Lewis's old Clapham Sect friend, reformer and MP for Yorkshire William Wilberforce. Having led the Parliamentary campaign against the slave trade until the passing of the *Slave Trade Act* of 1807 Wilberforce welcomed every opportunity to escape to the idyllic world of his fellow Evangelical and share his many dreams of Christian revival and discuss the prospects of the Jewish people.

The Slave Trade Act of 1807 had not yet brought slavery to an end but it would forbid British ships from carrying people who were to be sold into slavery and, in time, that would lead to the abolition of slavery in the British Empire in 1833, shortly before the death of Wilberforce. Meanwhile there were many social causes to be fought for and Wilberforce would respond in the spirit of his own maxim:

"You may choose to look the other way, but you can never say again that you did not know".[118]

The guest list at Stansted was nothing if not eclectic and Joseph Wolff[119] stands out not only as an amazing character but as one of the very few Jewish followers of Jesus of any stature to come out of the London Society at that time. He could not have been more different in character to William Wilberforce and yet they, and many others, found common ground in the totally committed but vulnerable, Lewis Way. Some years later Wolf would say of this "excellent man", that he was sometimes "disappointed and cheated by impostors".[120] That was probably an understatement.

Joseph was born in 1795, the son of a Rabbi, at Weilersbach near Saarbrücken, Germany, close to the French border. His parents, David and Sarah Levi, had named him Wolff at his circumcision but he would take Joseph as his Christian name when he was baptised and so would become Joseph Wolff. David and Sarah wanted the best for Wolff and hoped he would become a doctor but, as often happened at that time in Germany, the best modern education was to be found among the gentiles. And so he was sent to the Lutheran lyceum in Stuttgart, and later to

---

[118] "Having heard all of this, you may choose to look the other way, but you can never say again that you did not know." William Wilberforce, in a speech to Parliament against the slave trade, 12 May 1789

[119] Joseph Wolff (1795-1862)

[120] *Travels and Adventures of the Rev. Joseph Wolff D.D., LL.D.,* 1861

the Roman Catholic lyceum at Bamberg. Having read and been impressed by the Old Testament prophecies concerning Messiah Jesus in *Issiah 53*, at the age of just seven, this contact with the Christian world would lead him away from the Judaism of his family and draw him nearer to the faith he would retain for the rest of his life. Joseph Wolff was baptised in 1812 by Leopold Zolda the Benedictine Abbot of Emmaus, near Prague.

In 1819, having typically fallen out with the Roman Catholic Church over the doctrine of Papal infallibility he had been thrown out by the Inquisition. The terror tactics of the Inquisition, particularly the notorious Spanish Inquisition, had long been more or less abolished but the Inquisition remained a powerful force against perceived heresy in the Papal States and still reached deeply into the Catholic world under different names.

The totally unpredictable Wolff then turned up in London, still only twenty-four years old, and decided to become an Anglican under the influence of the Church of England liturgy he heard at the London Society's Bethnal Green headquarters, Palestine Place. In London he met up with the banker Henry Drummond, who he had known as a student in Rome. Drummond was one of the founders of the later discredited Catholic Apostolic or "Irvingite" Church. Leader Edward Irving's key themes were the imminent restoration of Israel and the Second Coming of Jesus, which appealed to the sometimes ingenuous Lewis Way. However, Irving insisted on setting a date for the Messiah's return, 1864, which would certainly not have appealed to Lewis[121]. Such unorthodox teaching on the end times and his heretical views on the humanity of Christ brought the Irvingite Church into disrepute and Irving himself to excommunication and isolation from the mainstream churches.

Drummond introduced Wolff to the Evangelical Charles Simeon, a founder of the London Society and senior minister at Holy Trinity Church, Cambridge.[122] Simeon would become Wolff's tutor and introduced him to Lewis Way who would become his patron. The scene was set for one of the most exiting Christian adventures since St Paul himself and it is all recounted, from shipwrecks to life-threatening illnesses, murderous encounters in the desert and amazing conversion experiences in his autobiography, *Travels and Adventures of the Rev. Joseph Wolff.*[123]

Joseph tells us, in the third person, as he dictates to an uncredited writer:

"In 1824 Wolff received 200 lashes, from the Kurds, in Mesopotamia"
"In the year 1827, Wolff's ship was wrecked, and he saved himself in a little boat"
"In the year 1830, Wolff was robbed by pirates near Salonica"
"In 1832, when they wanted to make Wolff into sausages, in Dooab (in the Hindoo-Kosh), but were ultimately satisfied with stripping him of every rag, and he arrived naked, like Adam and Eve, and even without an apron to cover himself"

And so on. But this was all yet to come.

---

[121] See Matthew 24:36
[122] from 1783 until his death in 1836
[123] *Travels and Adventures of the Rev. Joseph Wolff D.D., LL.D.,* 1861

Before meeting Lewis Way Wolff had already travelled widely in Europe and had acquired several languages but Lewis and Charles Simeon were keen for Joseph to complete his theological education in Cambridge, despite objections from Drummond. With growing freedom for non-conformist churches, especially in America, there were increasing opportunities for less formally educated and less well-off believers to find themselves in leadership positions as preachers and Free Church leaders. This was often a good thing and broadened the scope of the Church but, sadly this auto-didactic tendency also gave opportunities for some people to build their own churches in their own image. Such were Joseph Smith and the Mormons in 1820s and Charles Taze Russell and the Jehovah's Witnesses in the 1870s.

Way and Simeon, aware that Wolff was their star Jewish pupil, wanted him to be an academically sound Evangelist when they set him loose on the world! So many had let them down since Jacob Josephson ran off with the silver, and the return to the Land as born-again believers was proving less popular than they had expected among the comfortable Jews of England.

Chapter 19

Educating the mind without educating the heart is no education at all.

Aristotle

While Joseph Wolff pursued his theological training in Cambridge, Lewis Way turned his attention once more to the plan for a Royal Charter for his proposed Hebrew College at Stansted. He had become convinced, after much prayer, and not a little contradictory advice from his friends and family, that he really must comply with the spirit of John Way's generous gift.

He had called a meeting of his friends at the house of William Wilberforce at Marden Park, Surrey, shortly after his return from Aix-la-Chapelle in 1818 and on the evening of 31st December they convinced him that he must use the money in God's service and return to the vision he received at *A la Ronde* twenty years before, "for Lewis cherished the idea," wrote daughter Drusilla, "that the Jews, once converted, would become teachers in their turn of unenlightened Gentiles."

In summing up the meeting Charles Simeon, Lewis's friend and Joseph Wolff's tutor said:

"It was not a plan hastily taken up by Mr Way. God had laid it upon his heart many years ago, and now, after much deliberation and patience, instead of wavering he was more desirous than ever of having it realized. Mr Way's fortune was not an hereditary one, but was unexpectedly given to him by God, and the person who left it wished to have it employed in the promoting the glory of God."[124]

The money simply was not his to build a family dynasty at Stansted.

In a moving paragraph in her family history of 1930 Anna Marie Stirling wrote about the consecration of the Chapel at Stansted:

Lewis Way preached there on January 24 [1819], and the next day, the Feast of the Conversion of St Paul, the Bishops of Gloucester and St David's consecrated the Chapel and chapel yard. After the ceremony, when the house was full of guests, Lewis was missing; and at length his wife found him alone, kneeling before the altar in the newly consecrated chapel, while by his side was a paper in which he had solemnly dedicated Stansted and the estate to God, to be used as a College for the training of Jewish and foreign missionaries.[125]

Shortly afterwards, Lewis drew up a Petition which he sent to Prime Minister Robert Jenkinson, 2nd Earl of Liverpool, with a request that he would use his influence to procure the grant of a Royal Charter for the projected

---

[124] As recorded by Revd Charles Sleech Hawtrey, Canon of Exeter

[125] *The Ways of Yesterday*, A.M.W. Stirling, 1930 p. 199

Institution. He also sent a petition to Robert Burgess,[126] Bishop of St David's and Bishop of Salisbury and a staunch supporter of the London Society. In 1820 Burgess went so far as to obtain an interview with King George IV at Carlton House but, according to Lewis's daughter, he left behind the petition which Lewis had prepared along with the gift of a Hebrew Bible, also meant for the King.[127] In mitigation for this miserable failure the Bishop apparently observed that, "the Princess Augusta was present and was much interested."[128]

The charter was never to be granted. His friend and second cousin Charles Sleech Hawtrey[129] wrote:

"I had yesterday an interview with our two Bishops, Lichfield (late Gloucester) and St David's. I can in consequence send you some information which is of a definite nature. The Bishop of Lichfield first began by stating his full conviction that the Charter would never be granted by the Privy Council. Some would think it an urgent thing, some a mad thing, and others a Methodistic or Calvinistic thing; but pass it never would."[130]

Under the terms of a charter Lewis would wish to retain a measure of control and this was not acceptable to the Government or the Establishment.

---

[126] Burgess, Thomas (1756–1837)
[127] Nonetheless, possibly because he would not renounce all personal supervision of the proposed Institution, Lewis failed to obtain the requisite charter. *The Ways of Yesterday*, A.M.W. Stirling, 1930 p. 279
[128] The King's granddaughter, Princess Augusta Sophia (1768–1840) sixth child and second daughter of George III and Queen Charlotte.
[129] Charles Sleech Hawtrey (1780-1831)
[130] A.M.W. Stirling, *The Ways of Yesterday*, 1930

In 1821 the London Society established an Institution of its own called the Seminary. This was a less formal affair than Lewis's proposed Royal College and he generously invited them to his home in Stansted where they settled in Aldsworth House, one of the lodges on the estate until 1827. Lewis also presented his library of Hebrew and other Christian books to the Institution.[131]

In his 1908 history of the London Society W.T. Gidney[132] writes:

"In the first two years, of the eight students received, only two were Jewish converts, its primary object being the training of Gentile missionaries."

But he adds:

"In the Seminary at Stansted many of the famous early missionaries of the Society were trained for their future work"

This is a measure of Lewis Way's dedication to the Society, which would make the coming rift even more disastrous and tragic. Gidney describes Lewis as, "practically the founder of the Society as we know it." He had bailed them out with a massive donation when they faced bankruptcy in the early days.

---

[131] W.T. Gidney, *The History of the London Society for Promoting Christianity Amongst the Jews from 1809 to 1908*, 1908 p. 75
[132] William Thomas Gidney (1852-1909)

The achievement at the Aix-la-Chapelle Congress was a hard act for Lewis to follow. For now he was enjoying a certain amount of fame and was spending some time with his family. But he also undertook demanding preaching tours of England and Ireland as well as his prolific writing of poetry and prose and deputations for the London Society.

And so, in the autumn of 1822 the whole family, including baby Catherine Louisa, would leave Stansted for the Continent having let the family estate to John Julius Angerstein for two years. It would be a well-earned family holiday, but with a difference only Lewis Way would think of. The ladies would stay in Italy while Lewis and his son Albert, age seventeen, would take off for Jerusalem.

PART II

Chapter 20

"These pleasures are the last gasps of a society so lost in its escapism that it sickens you and makes you sympathetic to a revolutionary solution."

Jean Vigo on his film *A propos de Nice* (1930)

From 29 January 1820 the hedonistic Prince Regent finally became King George IV on the death of his 'mad' father. The portly prince adopted Brighton and its stony beach to be a fashionable spa resort on the grand European scale. His friend, the architect John Nash, who had created the 'Regency' style in London was engaged to design the prince's exotic Royal Pavilion with its extravagantly colourful Indian and Chinese interiors. The bright white oriental onion domes and Islamic style minarets of the Pavilion, vaguely based on the Taj Mahal, drew the fashionable and the wealthy to the heart of Brighton. The prince's personal seaside playground became the out-of-town centre of social life for the idle rich, and the not so idle rich like Lewis Way and his friend John Mortlock.

Over 100,000 people visited the resort every year and, before the arrival of the steam railway from London to Brighton in 1841, most of them travelled by coach on the dusty Sussex roads. One of the finest stagecoaches was the gleaming maroon and black *Brighton Comet* drawn by four strong horses travelling from London to Brighton in under six hours. Lewis and his family would frequently visit his favourite uncle John Baker Holroyd, 1st Earl of Sheffield. But when the sunshine left Brighton so did the idle rich, and they all headed south for Nice and the *Côte d'Azur*.

From 1815 until 1860 the French Mediterranean city we know as Nice, playground of the rich and near neighbour of St Tropez, was part of the Duchy of Savoy in the Kingdom of Piedmont-Sardinia. However, its colourful and complex history as part of pre-unification Italy made little difference to the wealthy English visitors who travelled through France to reach the Azur Coast and relief from the English weather. Such was the journey undertaken by Lewis Way and his family from Brighton as the severe winter of 1822-23 approached.[133]

The *Brighton Gleaner* of Monday 4 November 1822 reported in its sycophantic "Coorts (sic) and Fashionable" pages that:

This day fortnight[134], Mr Mortlock[135] whose benevolent disposition is known in all parts of the country, had the honour of an audience with the Duke of Cambridge. Mr Mortlock, the same afternoon, together with Mr and Mrs Lewis Way, left us for Dover, to embark for Calais, having in their retinue the

---

[133] 1822-23: Severe winter, ice on the Thames by late December. February 8th saw a great snowstorm in Northern England. People had to tunnel through the snow. D. Fauvell and I. Simpson, *The History of British Winters*

[134] Monday 21 October 1822

[135] Philanthropist John Mortlock (1776-1837) owner of the Mortlock China Company in Oxford Street, London.

celebrated travelling carriage of the late Corsican usurper of the throne of France. Mr Lewis Way purposes, it appeared, to remain some years in Paris, his object being to establish an English chapel there, and in which undertaking, it is said, he has the countenance of the Earl of Liverpoole (sic).

It is not clear which of Napoleon's carriages Lewis had purchased for the trip. It was not, as the *Gleaner* seemed to think, the Emperor's 'celebrated travelling carriage', his *dormeuse* or sleeper, which was left behind at Waterloo. Neither, according to Albert Way's drawing of the Nice convoy, was it the high speed *Berline* or Landau which was also abandoned on the battlefield. These were the only two *"voitures personnelles"* of Napoleon and they accompanied him everywhere in battle, one a high spec mobile-home, the other a lightweight model built for a fast getaway. Of the fourteen more regular carriages in the Emperor's *suite* of vehicles only nine made it back to Paris. One state carriage was exhibited as booty at London's Vauxhall Gardens and the other two are unaccounted for. One of those three seems to have been acquired by Lewis Way, possibly in Brussels on his return from Russia. It became the family coach and was known as 'the heavy.'

And so they set out for Nice, not Paris at this time as the *Gleaner* had announced, via Calais and the long road south. Leading the way was Lewis in an open top phaeton with his multilingual, musical daughter Drusilla, now a pretty and clever eighteen-year-old. This fast, sporty carriage was drawn by two horses and driven by a coachman and a postilion. Behind, but sometimes leading the way was the 'heavy.' Packed inside and outside of this Napoleonic motor-home were Mary Way, her four young daughters,

Albert and his tutor, Phesbey the governess, John the butler and Betty the cook.

From the port of Calais they headed down to the cathedral city of Reims, where the kings of France were crowned, through Picardy and Champagne-Ardennes to Dijon and the heart of the ancient Duchy of Burgundy. Thence through the vineyards of the Côte d'Or... Nuits-Saint-Georges, Mâcon, Beaune and Beaujolais to the 19th century silk centre of Lyon, gateway to the south. The late autumn sunshine warmed the endless fields of naked vines turning the sheltering leaves from yellow, to orange, and finally to brown. The curious cortège rode on, following the broad blue river Rhône, soon to be joined by the Saône, to Marseille and the bright azure Mediterranean coast road to Nice.

Although the 'heavy' was loaded to the gunwales with the necessities of a year's vacation some heavier items would follow them down by sea to be picked up at Nice. These included Drusilla's harp, Mary Way's Tomkinson piano, and the children's ponies! Sadly the ponies did not survive the bad weather. Ever optimistic, Mary wrote to her mother in Exeter:

Mr Mortlock, always on the watch to do what is liberal and kind, has sent us some china and two large tin boxes of London Biscuits and a casket of London Porter. The luggage is all arrived uninjured, the harp and new piano forte without a scratch, the latter a very sweet one, a patent Tomkinsons, chosen by Miss Way. The Devonshire hams arrived quite safely, which I scarcely expected, being packed three months and laying about in damp places; but except one (being nibbled by a mouse) which is for our Sunday's dinner tomorrow, they are uninjured.. . . It is curious that here wine, oil, apples, potatoes, bread and almost everything is sold by the pound. We have a great increase of livestock, several dogs being come (Pat among them) and two produced on the voyage.

At Nice the family party was joined by, among others, two of Lewis's sisters, Catherine, also known as Aunt Kitty, who in 1826 would marry Montague John Cholmeley and become Lady Cholmeley, and Mary Anne and her husband, the Revd Edward Whitby. The Revd Whitby would soon be making himself useful at Lady Olivia Sparrow's new English Chapel.

Chapter 21

Sometimes the valley below is like a bowl filled up with fog.
I can see hard green figs on two trees and pears on a tree just below me.
A fine crop coming in. May summer last a hundred years.

Frances Mayes, *Under the Tuscan Sun: At Home in Italy*, 1996

Lady Olivia Sparrow, "quite the guardian Angel of Nice", according to Mary Way in a letter to her mother, was a lady of considerable substance. She was the daughter of the second Viscount and first Earl of Gosford, wife of the late Brigadier-General Robert Sparrow of Worlingham Hall, Suffolk, who had died of a fever at sea, and possessor, in her lifetime, of very large amounts of property.

Married in 1797 and widowed just eight years later, Lady Sparrow was said to be a very eligible widow. One visitor from America even wrote home in 1824 that "Lady Olivia is a grandmother, yet is apparently quite young and beautiful." But the beautiful Olivia would never remarry, in all her eighty-eight years. Like so many others Olivia often left her country estate in England, the delightful Brampton Park in Huntingdonshire, and followed the sun southwards. But she was, far from idle, though very rich, and there was no relief from her commitment to education and other good works. Through the Vice Consul in Nice she distributed about seven hundred Bibles and Testaments amongst the poor who apparently only had access to the Scriptures in Latin. She also provided several hundred religious books to form a circulating library for the English, or English speaking residents and at one time she had a large school at Villa Franca, now Villefranche-sur-Mer, near Nice.

But Lady Olivia's crowning achievement in Nice was to fund half the English Chapel built in 1820-21 in memory of her son, Robert, who died in 1818 at Villa Franca. British residents and many visiting clergymen also contributed financially to the establishment of the Chapel. Trinity Anglican Church, Nice, a direct descendant of the chapel and on the same site, now on the busy *rue de la Buffa*, celebrated its 150th anniversary recently.

On their arrival in January 1823 Revd Lewis Way and his brother-in-law Revd Edward Whitby were appointed as the first clergymen of the new chapel and established an English speaking congregation there. Lewis's son Albert would return several times to the South of France and would die there, at Cannes, in 1874. In addition to his work as chaplain the generous Lewis helped many people, too many according to the usually accepting Mary. Writing home she says:

"People are plaguing Lewis for money. He has advanced £150 to one, and made an allowance to another for 3 or 4 years."

He funded, with others, the building of the famous *Promenade des Anglais*. It was ostensibly built in order to give work to the many beggars who appeared in the town when the English arrived but also, of course, for the benefit of Lewis's many friends in the town who could enjoy the three mile *promenade* along the Mediterranean seafront in the cool of the evening. He would become known locally by the pejorative title of *Louis d'Or*, after the valuable gold coin, but it probably didn't bother him too much.

Back in London the Society had been keen to send a team to investigate the Jewish presence along the coast of the Mediterranean, also to ascertain the facilities for establishing a College in the neighbourhood of Mount Lebanon, and finally to visit Jerusalem. Lewis was their man and they were anxious for him to start work. He would be accompanied by William Buckmore Lewis, an Irish member of the London Society. The plan was to visit Jerusalem at Passover on 27 March 1823, when large numbers of Jewish people would be in town for the festival. Lewis no doubt saw this as an opportunity to speak to a Jewish assembly on its own territory and to announce the Messiah's coming and the Second Coming, all within sight of the Mount of Olives.

Lewis's protégé, Joseph Wolff had already reached Jerusalem via Lebanon in March of 1822 and reported regularly to the London Society's publication, *The Jewish Expositor and Friend of Israel*. His exciting tales and adventures no doubt gripped the readers of the *Expositor* as they can still grip the reader today. Wolff, a totally committed Jewish believer in Jesus, was an extraordinary man with a vast vision and a seemingly dauntless character. But he was not, it would seem, the right man for the mission the London Society had in mind.

Lewis Way, for all his own foibles, was a reliable envoy for the Society. Wolff could be unpredictable and would often run out of funds which the Society seemed unwilling, or unable to provide. Lewis was self-financing and could be relied on to establish mission stations and make useful connections with his social background and communication skills. In other words, Lewis was a great networker and fundraiser.

And so the plan was that he should start his journey from the port of Naples in a vessel called the *Hebe* in the spring of 1823. The *Hebe*, a three-master transport vessel, had just returned from Australia as a convict ship, dropping off 159 male prisoners at Sydney, New South Wales. The *Hebe* sailed from England on 31st July 1820, arrived in Sydney, on 31st December. She arrived back in England on 23rd January 1822 and was chartered by Lewis to pick his team up at Naples. The ship arrived three days late giving them time to relax and visit the Roman towns of Pompeii and Herculaneum, disastrously engulfed in the eruption of Mount Vesuvius in AD 79.

When the *Hebe* arrived the plan was that Albert Way would stay with Lewis Way and Revd William Buckmore Lewis would head for Jerusalem to represent the London Society. They would take large quantities of Bibles and other literature which they would take on board at Malta. Lewis Way refers to "10,000 Bibles on the shore of the Holy Land"[136] but this has been disputed and a smaller figure suggested which may have included other gospel material

---

[136] *Jewish Expositor and Friend of Israel, volume 9, 1829*

from London.[137] This may well just have been hyperbole on the part of Lewis the poet referring to a long-term hope with this smaller delivery as just the beginning. But, under the circumstances it seems quite likely that as many as 10,000 Bibles *were* put on board the *Hebe* at Valletta. This, like most things Lewis undertook, was a big project.

Missionary William Jowett[138] "had established a printing facility in Malta that became a centre for Bible translation and distribution."[139] The Malta Bible Society's work began in 1810 and they formally associated themselves with the British and Foreign Bible Society in 1817. At that time they appear to have concentrated on the Italian language, being "the most general medium of communication in the Mediterranean." But by 1821 the ubiquitous Joseph Wolff, working for the British and Foreign Bible Society, was in contact with the Malta Bible Society and wrote to them from the British Consulate in Cairo on 21st December 1821 regarding the "twelve Greek and two Arabic New Testaments, two Hebrew Bibles, twelve Arabic Psalters, and three Hebrew Psalters" he was taking to the convent on Mount Sinai. Joseph took three camels, the third of which was "laden with the trunks of Bibles and Testaments." The monks at Sinai asked Wolff if he could provide more copies of the Arabic New Testament. He also requests German Bibles and Testaments, "fifty copies would not be too many," he wrote. Such was the determination of this extraordinary man.

---

[137] *Mishkan - A Forum on the Gospel and the Jewish People*, Issue 55, 2008 p. 60

[138] William Jowett (1787-1855)

[139] *Biographical Dictionary of Christian Missions*, edited by Gerald H. Anderson 1998

Clearly the Malta Bible Society could now provide, either from their own presses or from outside sources, Bibles or parts of the Bible in many other Mediterranean languages. The London Society had also sent Testaments and Tracts to Malta for Lewis to collect. Lewis Way was a dreamer, but he knew by faith how to make dreams come true. Mary Way and her daughters meanwhile were to await their return in a Villa at Lucca in Tuscany. But before all this Lewis determined to take his unmarried sister (Aunt Kitty) and two elder children (Drusilla and Albert) on a tour through Italy, after which Drusilla and her aunt were to re-join Mary while Lewis, son Albert and William Buckmore Lewis embarked for Syria.

Following some complicated logistics with Mary and the children Lewis, William and Albert found their way to the *Hebe* at Naples via Florence and Rome, with an unexpected visit to Pompeii and Herculaneum. The two ladies, Kitty and Drusilla joined them on the visit to Florence and Rome leaving the Eternal City to return to Leghorn on 1st May 1823 with Mr 'Nos' Nosworthy. That was as far east as respectable Georgian ladies could go, although Lewis was soon to meet a lady who did not recognise that barrier, or any other rules concerning the role of women, the formidable Lady Hester Stanhope. Mary Way, the children and the staff had to make do with a hot summer in Tuscany where the ladies ended up until October when they were all to be reunited in Leghorn and head for Paris. Part of Lewis's plan in leasing Stansted for two years had been to spend the second year in Paris as the *Brighton Gleaner* had prematurely announced. But more of that later. With the ladies settled in Tuscany the real mission could begin in earnest.

Chapter 22

"Many that live deserve death. And some that die deserve life. Can you give it to them? Then do not be too eager to deal out death in judgement. For even the very wise cannot see all ends."

J.R.R. Tolkien, *The Fellowship of the Ring, Book I, Chapter 2 (Gandalf)*

American evangelists Pliny Fisk[140] and Jonas King[141], were returning from a two month mission in Jerusalem having left behind their new found brother, our old friend Joseph Wolff, who had unfinished business in the city. They had distributed a hundred New Testaments and five thousand tracts and were approaching the port of Sidon in Lebanon.......

"On coming in sight of the latter place [Sidon] they spied an English ship of considerable size anchored off the town, which proved most unexpectedly to be a missionary ship commanded by a pious ex-admiral of the British navy, chartered and employed expressly to bring to these shores two English missionaries. They had come under the auspices of the London Jews' Society. One of them was the Rev. Lewis Way, a gentleman of wealth and engaged with much enthusiasm in the Jewish cause. He had left Sidon by land, and was occupying himself in fitting up an

---

[140] Pliny Fisk (1792-1825)
[141] Jonas King (1792-1869)

establishment for himself and his fellow-labourers in the vicinity of Beirut. His associate, however, the Rev. Mr Lewis, was still at Sidon, and with him they spent a very agreeable Sabbath."[142]

The "English ship of considerable size" was the *Hebe*. She had arrived at Sidon on 21st May 1823 from Naples and was due back in County Cork, Ireland to pick up emigrant settlers for passage to Quebec on 8th July. It can only be assumed that Lewis chartered such a big ship in order to cross the Mediterranean with his precious cargo of Bibles without fear of sinking, running aground or having the cargo thrown overboard. Such events were not uncommon but the *Hebe* was an ocean-going vessel and would take the Med in its stride. The return journey, however, might not be so comfortable....Lewis had only booked a one way trip on the *Hebe*.

He had hoped to land at Joppa (Jaffa, Israel) and travel the thirty-seven miles by land to Jerusalem, but he heard the plague had broken out in the city and in Alexandria so he decided to land at Sidon to the north in Lebanon and journey straight to Beirut leaving William Buckmore Lewis with the ship. To his great delight, while resting at a monastery near the coast, Lewis encountered his old friend and protégée Joseph Wolff, then on his way to Damascus. The usually indefatigable Joseph told Lewis about an encounter he had with Lady Hester Stanhope, to whom Lewis had a letter of introduction, who had "hounded"

---

[142] *Bible Work in Bible Lands, Events in the History of the Syrian Mission,* Revd Isaac Bird, 1872

him out of Syria. Such was the apparent power of this notorious Englishwoman.

Who was this tyrant who could, apparently, distress a man who had been captured, beaten, robbed and had often faced death for his faith? What kind of ogre could scare an evangelist who had been whipped, shipwrecked, and left to die in the desert? The culprit was one Hester Lucy Stanhope.

Victorian preacher Catherine Marsh in a letter to Caroline Fuller-Maitland would write that she had read about Lady Hester Stanhope, "with mingled interest, amusement, and disgust." And Lewis's cynical daughter wrote:

"Dad has introduced to a Monastery at Lebanon[143] and likewise to Lady Hester from Lady Bute; but which it is supposed will not be much use, as she is very averse to seeing her own countryfolk and lives continually with her favourite Arab in tents on the mountains."

But Hester was keen to meet this fellow countryman who had committed so much to achieving the long-awaited return of the Jews to the Land of Israel. Hester believed she would play a major part in what she saw as the imminent mass exodus to *Eretz Yisrael*, the Land of Israel. The much maligned, and misunderstood Hester was born 12th March 1776, the only daughter of Charles Stanhope, Viscount Mahon, 3rd Earl Stanhope (1753-1816) and Hester

---

[143] Lewis, along with Drusilla, had been introduced to Pope Pius VII on their visit to Rome. The Pope, a great Anglophile since the defeat of Napoleon, offered him helpful contacts in Lebanon through Cardinal Gonsalvi.

Pitt (1755-1780) at the beautiful three thousand acre family estate of Chevening House, near Sevenoaks in Kent. As we are only concerned here with her dealings with Lewis Way and his millennial mission, at a time when Hester would be nearly fifty years old, we must pass over her childhood and youth, except to say that she was a very intelligent and perceptive child. Her exciting and truly dramatic life is very well recounted in Kirsten Ellis's 2008 biography, *Star of the Morning, The Extraordinary Life of Lady Hester Stanhope*.

As a young lady in high society Hester was not a great beauty in any conventional, fashionable sense, but by the power of the subtle good looks she undoubtedly had, as well as her charismatic presence and, above all, her understanding of the nature of power, she would be attracted to, and by, powerful men. Her uncle was no less a man than Prime Minister William Pitt the Younger (1759-1806) and she would become what Lewis Way calls Pitt's "intimate and confidential manager," in the course of time. During that bitter time of war with France and Napoleon there could be no more useful introduction to the world of political intrigue and power for a young woman than this.

Although she would consider marriage and had several serious *liaisons*, matrimony was never to be part of her unconventional life. Her equally unconventional religious views probably began with her rejection of Christianity as represented by the authority of the Church of England. At an early age she refused to be confirmed in the Anglican Church and would not be persuaded otherwise. By the time she met Lewis Way in Lebanon she had evolved a religion of her own rather like some modern 'pick and mix' religions of today. Surrounded as she was by Sufi dervishes, the Yezidi and their astral spirits, Sufism, Cabalism as well as several variants of Islam her enquiring mind wandered around this supermarket of faith and rejected Christianity for good.

She was, however, attracted to Lewis Way's well-known prophetic ministry as being somehow related to the prophecy given to her in her youth. During her time with Pitt the Younger a self-proclaimed prophet called Richard Brothers, who was being held in Newgate prison, insisted, before being transferred to a lunatic asylum, that he speak to the young Lady Hester. He told her that she would spend seven years in the Middle East and would be the one to lead the Jewish people back to the Land of Israel.

Like so many misguided prophecies which come from an 'unreliable' source, there was an element of truth in this because Hester, on a journey of discovery through the Ottoman Empire, would decide to stay in Lebanon partly on the strength of that prophecy. Thus it was a kind of self-fulfilling prophecy of no real value, as Lewis would realise in time. His own interpretations of Bible prophecy, particularly in the Book of Revelation, did not feature her Ladyship as playing a major part in the end times scenario. In addition to all the other spiritual influences in her life she had for over twenty years supported a Frenchman named Loustaunau who had been a General of Tippoo Sahib in India.[144] He was also known to Hester as "The

---

[144] Tippoo Sahib (1750-1799) also known as the Tiger of Mysore was a ruler of the Kingdom of Mysore and a scholar, soldier and poet.

Prophet" and claimed to have predicted the great earthquake of 1822 in that region.

Such was the bizarre world of Hester Lucy Stanhope when Lewis Way called to pay his respects. But, whatever Hester was, she was not insane as some supposed. She was eccentric, she was brave, she was reckless, but she wasn't mad. It was all too easy to declare somebody mad at that time, often an unwanted wife, and all too easy to find doctors to support the false diagnosis and have them put away. But Hester did have a fearful temper and she did send the gentle Joseph Woolf packing when he had only called in with a letter from Malta for her companion and maid of honour, Miss Williams. According to Isaac Byrd, author of *Bible Work in Bible Lands* in 1872:

"Miss Williams replied that she had her positive orders not to have any communication with him, and that her ladyship was thinking of issuing a circular to all her friends in the land respecting these "wandering gentlemen," to say that her ladyship disowned them all."

Her Ladyship added the following regarding Joseph's Jewish roots:

"I am astonished that an apostate should dare to thrust himself into observation in my family. Had you, whose real name I know not, been a learned Jew, never could you have abandoned a religion rich in itself, yet defective, to embrace a shadow of one. Light travels faster than sound; therefore the Supreme Being could never have allowed his creatures to remain in utter darkness for nearly two thousand years, until paid speculating

146

wanderers might think it proper to lift their venal voice to enlighten them.

When Joseph sent a courteous reply to this the messenger was whipped and beaten by her Ladyship before being sent back and could only be consoled by the gift of a silver dollar from Joseph.

Hester Stanhope's other great dream was the unification of the Arab people against the power of the Ottoman Empire. This was nearly a century before the legendary Lawrence of Arabia made his own contribution to that cause. But neither of them succeeded in uniting the tribes' ancient differences permanently, and by the time Lewis arrived at Djoun Hester had become a virtual prisoner in her own fortress mountain home having backed the wrong side in a major tribal war. It was only her perceived mystical powers which kept her from being killed by the superstitious tribesmen.

So Lewis did not arrive at a very convenient time. The vast house was chaotic and devoid of Hester's beautiful furniture and fittings which had been stolen by the servants and others when Hester was near to death with the plague. But because of her secretive nature Lewis may not have been aware of her condition or all the reasons for her reduced circumstances. She had sheltered and assisted many victims of the war, on both sides.

He would spend a few days with Hester being subjected to what her physician and biographer[145] would call "those

---

[145] Charles Lewis Meryon (1783–1877)

interminable conversations which filled so large a portion of her time, and seemed so necessary to her life."[146] Hester could hold an almost one-way conversation with her guests for anything up to twelve hours, such was the intensity of her mind. Lewis gleaned that Lady Hester now lived in expectation of a great 'Deliverer', whom some called the Haken, some the Mahedi, some the Messiah, and that he would execute the last judgments on the wicked by famine, pestilence, battle, murder and sudden death, during which the just would be preserved and finally established in the Holy Land on the restoration of the Jews, led by herself. Lewis would write with some restraint to Mary:

"Lady Hester is preparing for these events on the dry ground of tradition and opinion, not what a Christian should do, who has a more sure word of Prophecy."

He left convinced that Lady Hester was losing the plot and was muddled and confused as so many others would be as they moved away from Bible-based truth, looking into mysticism and interpreting prophecy in terms of their own ego. Many sects would be born out of this fundamental misunderstanding as the free-thinking 19th century rolled on. Whatever interpretation Lewis might put on Bible prophecy he knew it always referred to Jesus, and only Jesus, as the resurrected Messiah and unique source of salvation: Jesus said, "I am the way and the truth and the life. No one comes to the Father except through me." (John 14:6). It was Jesus himself who would "come again, with

---

[146] *Memoirs of The Lady Hester as related by herself in conversations with her physician*, 1845

glory to judge both the quick and the dead: Whose Kingdom will have no end."[147] The details of time and place might be disputed but Jesus would not require any help and he would draw the Jewish people back to himself *by* himself. They would not be led or 'converted.'

Having called on Lady Hester, by this time unofficially known as the Queen of the East, Lewis, as a stickler for correct form, arranged to present himself and his son to the real ruler of Mount Lebanon, the ruthless Emir Bashir II[148]who would allow them to travel freely in his land. Prince Bashir had converted from Sunni Islam to become a Maronite Christian,[149] but this short-term benefit to Lewis would fade away as the Maronite church and the Jesuits reacted against American evangelicals, known as the "Bible Men," infiltrating Lebanon.

And so Lewis and son found themselves in Beirut with the Emir's temporary blessing. His partner, William Buckmore Lewis set out for Jerusalem having presumably been told by the Americans, Fisk and King, that it was safe to go there. Fisk and King then moved on to Beirut and would eventually meet up with Lewis Way at the monastery at Antoura. Lewis would acquire this former residence of the Jesuits, known as the Saint Joseph College of Antoura, and would take possession on 28th June 1823 with a view to establishing a Jewish College or Mission there in the future.

---

[147] Nicene creed - *Book of Common Prayer* 1662

[148] Emir Bashir Shihab II (1767-1850) ruler of Lebanon in the first half of the 19th century.

[149] The Maronite church remains to this day in communion with the Roman Catholic Church.

CHAPTER 23

We must accept finite disappointment, but never lose infinite hope.

Martin Luther King Jr

Turn off the 1,285 mile Beirut to Tripoli coastal highway at Zouq Mikael and drive up Mount Lebanon to the *Collège Saint Joseph* at Antoura and you will see the view that Lewis Way had over the deep blue Mediterranean Sea. Antoura lies between the mountains and the sea at an altitude of 250 to 300 metres above sea level. The college was, and is set among vineyards and groves of almonds and olives, surrounded by carob and pine trees, making it an idyllic setting for a college campus.

Lewis Way had finally arrived on Mount Lebanon and must have felt his mission had nearly been accomplished. He had raised £230 while he was in Nice and had set up a "Palestinian fund" at home.[150] The Lazarist Fathers[151] who had run the St Joseph College since 1783 under the ill-fated Louis XVI of France had let the place go since the French Revolution and were happy, at the time, to lease it to the

[150] W.T. Gidney, *The History of the London Society for Promoting Christianity Amongst the Jews from 1809 to 1908*, 1908 p. 118
[151] Founded by St Vincent de Paul and established at St Lazare in Paris, 1625

wealthy Englishman. Lewis settled in and began to plan the future of the mission. He writes:

"For several days I found great delight in visiting the most inaccessible and most romantic regions of this celebrated mountain, and many were the hopes I encouraged, the plans I formed, and the prayers I poured forth for future usefulness on this spot."

But his joy was to be short-lived. Within a few days Lewis was bed-ridden with what he called "an inflammatory eruption" in his legs. He was forced to lie on three boards made of pine and, as the heat of summer increased he became feverish and would later write:

".....my strength failed, my whole frame began to waste considerably, so that I was rendered utterly incapable of exertion mentally or bodily."

He would remain at the college for the whole of July, unable to move, sometimes looking out from his couch to the Mediterranean and across to distant Italy where his family awaited news of his mission.

By August Lewis was so weak he had decided he must return to France or possibly die in the gradually rising temperature of the Lebanese summer. Before he departed his growing depression was relieved by the arrival of his friend Joseph Wolff and the two Americans. They proposed to carry on the work at Antoura if Lewis had to leave and soon William Buckmore Lewis, who had been studying Arabic at Sidon also arrived and would spent some months in the college by way of preparation for future work.

On the 2nd of August 1823, Lewis and his son set sail on a Genoese boat from Sidon. Had he known that within a year or so the college would be abandoned under pressure from groups opposing the "Bible Men" his poor health may not have seen him through the horrendous journey to come. At the end of 1824 the London Society reported that:

"He [William Buckmore Lewis] spoke also of many difficulties caused by the Turkish and Roman Catholic prohibitions against circulating the Scriptures and preaching in Syria, and he was compelled to surrender the premises at Antoura."[152]

By the time Lewis and Albert left Sidon for Italy the *Hebe*, the ship that had taken them across the Mediterranean to Lebanon was sailing for Quebec, Canada. Lewis had not planned a return journey because he had no idea how the trip would go. In the event it went quite badly and he needed to get out fast and accepted passage on any ship that was willing to face the inconvenience of quarantine regulations at various ports on the Mediterranean, not to mention the risk of infection from the last days of the Cholera Pandemic of 1817-1823. Bubonic plague was also said to be breaking out in some areas of the Middle East but the plague was sometimes confused with cholera in historic reports. The last significant outbreak of the plague in Europe had been in Marseille in 1720 when it was carried to the city from the port of Sidon, but cholera

[152] W.T. Gidney, *The History of the London Society for Promoting Christianity Amongst the Jews from 1809 to 1908*, 1908

would, in spite of strict quarantine, menace Europe right up to the start of the twentieth century.

Lewis and his son do not seem to have been very good sailors which, along with Lewis's sickness, may have aggravated Albert's dramatic reports of the journey. The first problem was the crew. They spoke a language the Ways did not understand, a seemingly obscure *patois* that could not be interpreted by way of French or Italian, or Latin. English at that time was not usually an option. They only knew they were headed for the port Livorno in rough weather. They had paid the Master handsomely, not only for the trip but for any periods of quarantine, and the health risk. But he may not have passed their generosity on to his crew.

Next, the food fell short of expectations for a Mediterranean cruise and Lewis says:

"We had nothing to eat but stale bread, common rice and the starved poultry of Syria."

Which was probably what most Genoese sailors ate at the time and, running the gauntlet of the deadly cholera, they were probably disinclined to serve anything better to their English passengers. After several days they longed to reach the Maltese port of Valetta but adverse winds kept them away and they were forced to land at Syracuse in Sicily where quarantine was in force. But they were back on land and they were back in Europe, though still a long way from Leghorn and the family. Lewis takes comfort from the homely voice of the local British representative..........

153

"......that which refreshed me most was the sound of an English voice and the tidings of modern Europe, which I collected from the English Consul, with whom I was only permitted to converse......through a strong fence and at a distance of several feet, for this is all the intercourse allowed to fresh comers from Syria."

At the end of the quarantine period they set sail for Leghorn (Livorno) without further disaster, but they faced a further period of forty days isolation in the Leghorn *lazaretto* or quarantine station before they could move on to Nice.

By the end of 1823 the risk of infection was probably very low and so Mary Way and two daughters were allowed to join Lewis and Albert in quarantine. As a result of overcrowding they were released after only twenty-five days on 22 October 1823 and planned their journey back to Nice. Mary would sail to Nice on the brig *Anitciziaas* while Lewis, still recovering from his seven weeks of sailing, would travel overland on his Arabian horse with Drusilla on what Mary calls her Bedouin. Aunt Kitty's mount is unidentified. The brig was a fast, manoeuvrable ship with two square-rigged masts and the journey should have been quick if uncomfortable as the winter weather approached. But, in the event, when they were just thirty miles off the coast of Nice the notorious Sirocco wind from the Sahara forced them to take shelter and land at Vado Ligure, on the wrong side of the Alps.

The next day, on the advice of the Captain they decided to travel overland from Vado to Nice via Savona and the 1,870 metre high *Col de Tende* mountain pass. The Captain could not guarantee sailing again for several days, so they landed their carriage and luggage at Vado and set off on the mountain roads for the fleshpots of Nice in the kingdom of Piedmont-Sardinia.

On their safe arrival at Nice on 8th November 1823, Mary wrote home:

"Lewis's beautiful Arabian carried him delightfully, and Drusilla's Bedouin, though she had never carried a lady before, is so tractable and quiet that she mounted her without a fear, and rode the chief part of the journey, and they arrived here quite safe and dear Lewis in much improved looks."

They would winter in Nice but by 3 May 1824 Lewis and Albert were in Paris and Lewis told Mary he would wait for her there. A very serious matter had come up with the London Society which was to affect the rest of their lives but he was not willing to travel to London to discuss it.

In a rare moment of public concern for Mary he writes to the London Society:

"I have now promised Mrs Way to wait for her at Paris, and I have far too often distressed and tried her affection to disappoint her now...."

Mary and Drusilla left Nice on Tuesday 24 May 1824 stopping over at Lyons from where they would journey to Orleans and await instructions from Lewis. They would meet Lewis either in Paris or Tours, where his brother George lived with his wife Susannah.

Chapter 24

That the Jews will return to their fatherland we are assured by numerous prophecies; but, perhaps, by none more distinctly than those which we find recorded in Zechariah 8:7 and 8, and also in Ezekiel 37: 21. Whether their conversion (predicted in Zechariah 12:10-14) is to precede, or follow their restoration; or whether there is to be a second appearing of Christ, or a great outpouring of the Holy Spirit upon them, we will not inquire: it is enough for us to know that God has promised their restoration and conversion.[153]

Ridley Herschell (1807-1864)

Lewis Way and the London Society For Promoting Christianity Amongst the Jews had fallen out over prophecy and the end of the world as we know it. To be accurate the Gloucester branch of the Society had fallen out with Lewis by complaining to the London office that he was making far too much, however eruditely, of end times theology, or eschatology. It cannot be denied that page after page of debate in the Society's magazine, the *Jewish Expositor and Friend of Israel* under his transparent *nom de plume* of Basilicus, was closely followed by page after endless page of replies from equally erudite

---

[153] From a sermon delivered on Sunday evening, February 5, 1843, at Chadwell Street Chapel, Islington, by the Rev R.H. Herschell.

correspondents. This was particularly true in the 1822 and 1823 editions and by 1824 some readers, particularly it seems in Gloucester, were tiring of it. They do not seem to have been tired of the debate *per se* which was very interesting to those who could follow it, but they were concerned that so much emphasis on the end times might detract from the simple gospel message, particularly as directed to Jewish people, which was a central *raison d'être* of the Society. Not that Jews could not understand the debate but, the Gloucester contingent argued, they needed to recognise Jesus as their long-awaited Messiah before the arguments had any meaningful context. This was never going to be easy, given the Church's appalling track record with the Jewish people, so the Society really should major on sharing the simple gospel message and the Jewish roots of Christianity with them.

The end, it has to be said, had been nigh for a long time even in Lewis's day but there were, and still are, really only two ways of looking at the end of the world for a Christian, however far off or near it may be. Firstly, the simple 'wait and see' approach. Jesus said,

"Because of the increase of wickedness, the love of most will grow cold, but he who stands firm to the end will be saved. And this gospel of the kingdom will be preached in the whole world as a testimony to all nations, and then the end will come." Matthew (24:12-14)

There seems to be no sure way of assessing the level or intensity of wickedness that will be in the world before the end comes, but we must simply "stand firm" and preach the gospel. The book of Revelation (Apocalypse) makes it clear that things *will* get much worse before they get better, but Jesus had already said that. And what about Jesus's return, the so-called Second Advent? Luke has the simple answer:

"They were looking intently up into the sky as he was going, when suddenly two men dressed in white stood beside them. "Men of Galilee," they said, "why do you stand here looking into the sky? This same Jesus, who has been taken from you into heaven, will come back in the same way you have seen him go into heaven." Acts 1:10-11

The second way of looking at the end of the world for a Christian is to spend a lot of time studying prophecy and gleaning, by whatever means, the smallest detail of the end times and join in the endless debate surrounding Dispensationalism and Millennialism. Such an exercise is clearly irresistible to many and, in itself, is presumably harmless and can add to our sum total of understanding. But when it leads to speculation about times and dates, as with Edward Irving, we must always remember what Jesus said:

"But about that day or hour no one knows, not even the angels in heaven, nor the Son, but only the Father." (Mark 13:32)

Lewis clearly had a firm foot in both camps but it was the prophecy that often got him misunderstood, and sometimes into trouble. For instance the Scottish preacher Thomas Guthrie[154] on hearing Lewis preach would write in his Paris journal in 1827:

---

[154] Thomas Guthrie (1803-1873)

"Way's sermon was most decidedly orthodox, and ably conceived and executed. He is rather eccentric in his manner of expressing himself, and too much given to fanciful speculations upon the prophecies of the Apocalypse, He seems to be infected with the same disease as Edward Irving - a mania of prophecy - interpreting, from which I cannot see the probability of any good results."

Of course Lewis had no way of knowing what the future held in detail and the machinations of Napoleon Bonaparte, however evil, would be overtaken by the pointless slaughter of the First World War and the near destruction of the Jewish people in the Holocaust. But Lewis knew the rules and he would defend himself against his detractors with the almost innocently simple argument that:

"If they can prove me wrong out of the Bible, I will own my error, but to silence discussion by authority is not the Protestant mode of establishing truth."[155]

But the leadership was adamant, Lewis must desist, and so he resigned immediately as a Vice-Chairman of the Society. The precocious Drusilla, now twenty years old and perhaps a bit miffed that her father did not consult *her* while they had been together so long in recent times, writes to her brother Albert in Paris from Lyon on 11th May 1824:

"I confess that it was painful to me, because it is so completely cutting all his former acquaintance and pursuits, and will bring

[155] *The Ways of Yesterday*, A.M.W. Stirling, 1930, p. 272

such an imputation of fickleness on him from those who will not enter into his real reasons.... I think being so near home he might have returned and consulted the Bishops and other friends before sending his congé to the Society."

Lewis would not travel to London; he was not only waiting for Mary to arrive but was running out of funds. He writes dramatically and in a spirit of martyrdom to the Society from Paris:

"I entreat you for God's sake, and for the Cause sake, and for nay life's sake (if that were of any consequence) think not of my coming to your meeting. Your Society has had my time and property and undivided attention for upwards of twelve years. . . . You have no right to take my life which would certainly be endangered by my coming over now as I fully intended."

He then adds, rather by way of an anti-climax:

"I have another reason . . . unless you or dear Thomas [Baring] will lend me one or two thousand pounds for a few months, I know not where to get the means of arranging my affairs. . . ."

About this time, shortly before the family left for Italy, Mary's uncle, probably William Rose Drewe, who was unmarried and had no children, died and left Mary a fortune:

".....the residue of which alone represented £25,000; while both to Drusilla and her father he left considerable legacies."

This seems to have been the funds Lewis was waiting for, which would guarantee a bridging loan from Baring.

Lewis seems to have spent £10,000 of this inheritance on buying the
Hôtel Marbeuf on the Avenue des Champs-Élysées. It would remain in the Way family until 1883 when the Paris city authorities acquired it for road widening:

"....compensation of twelve thousand pounds was given to the Way family, judged the legal owners of the site. The family gave this sum to the appeal for the building of a new church."[156]

Meanwhile, in a last ditch attempt to placate Lewis, Charles Sleech Hawtrey and William Marsh representing the London Society journeyed to Paris confident of overruling his decision, but they found him "adamant against their representations". He had supported the society and set it on its feet, but now he had a new vision and Paris would become the Way family's new home and, in time, their only home.

[156] *An Anglican Adventure – The History of St George's Anglican Church, Paris* – Matthew Harrison, 2005, p. 34

Chapter 25

Paris is always a good idea.

Audrey Hepburn

If you should find yourself walking, or promenading, down the Champs-Élysées in Paris and you have a few moments to spare, stop outside Le Rendez-Vous Toyota at number seventy-nine, opposite Marks & Spencer's at one hundred. Close your eyes and imagine yourself back nearly two hundred years to the chilly morning of Sunday 11th February 1827. You will be standing outside Lewis Way's new church, the Marbeuf Chapel, on the corner of rue de Chaillot now rue Quentin-Bauchart. Listen carefully and you may hear him preaching from the high pulpit to a thousand English visitors and expatriates *"of which description there are said to be usually not less than 20,000 in Paris."*[157] Sitting inside the church is the bluff Scottish Presbyterian minister and philanthropist Thomas Guthrie, who would later record Lewis's sermon in his journal:

"I had hardly got myself arranged when I was struck with the preacher's loud defiance to all atheists, infidels, Socinians, and scoffers at the Gospel, to prove the contrary of what he maintained. I thought I had fallen on my feet now, and so set myself for profound attention, which was immediately fixed by

---

[157] *Christian Spectator Conducted by an Association of Gentlemen, for the year 1826,* New Haven and New York

the preacher declaring, - in the tones of a man who is maintaining the truth - the object he had always had in view in what he had preached, wrought, and written. Then, striking on the Bible which lay before him (for he had no paper), "I find these doctrines there," and then, beating his breast, "I have felt them in my own heart!" Having, in proof of some position or another, referred to the case of Philip and the eunuch, he said, "Ay, it would be well that we followed the example of this eunuch - that, when travelling from one city to another, we employed ourselves in reading the Scriptures."

I was so well pleased with this touch, that I took out my box for a snuff, and made such a horrid noise (the people paying such profound attention) that I had three or four real British faces instantly fixed in wonderment on me. I, however, no ways abashed, took my pinch, quite delighted with my situation; and in a little time heard him declare that the end of all things was near at hand; that at present, as in the time of righteous Noah, the world was lying in wickedness, and particularly the cities of continental Europe; that, as the antediluvian inhabitants asked where were the waters that were to float the mighty bark which was built on the dry and solid earth, so the scoffers and practical infidels of our day now ask, "Where is the promise of His coming?" Then, raising himself up, and, prophet-like, stretching out his arm, he declared, "He shall come like a thief in the night. The very waters which once rolled their mighty tide over this earth shall be decomposed, and shall they roll over you, scoffers and worldly men and unbelievers, their flood of devouring fire!"

Lewis had clearly not lost his enthusiasm for fire and brimstone preaching, and people came in droves to hear him.

Until Lewis arrived in Paris from his aborted trip to the Middle East there had been no formal Anglican church in that predominantly Catholic city. Church of England services were conducted in the drawing room and ballroom of the British Ambassador's residence in the rue du Faubourg St Honoré, purchased by the Duke of Wellington, who was Ambassador to the restored Bourbon monarchy in 1814. But it could only cater for about three hundred people, most of whom would be from the upper classes, leaving no room for their many servants and staff.

Lewis it seems had planned to move to Paris for some time. It was not only cheaper, as his cash flow situation worsened, but he felt called to the spiritual needs of the large, predominantly English, expatriate community there. It is clear from the rather confused report in the *Brighton Gleaner* of 4 November 1822 on their departure for Italy, nearly two years before the opening of the Marbeuf Chapel, that Lewis was planning to live and work in Paris for some time:

"Mr Lewis Way purposes, it appeared, to remain some years in Paris, his object being to establish an English chapel there."

It was also clear that the vast estate at Stansted was becoming unsustainable. Mortgages and other debts meant Lewis knew in his heart the family home would have to be sold soon after the two year lease held by John Julius Angerstein expired. Following the long and bloody war with France, Paris was once again very popular with the wealthy British, who were generally known at the time by the generic term *les Anglais* whether Irish, Scottish, Welsh or English.[158] It was good to get back to the fashionable Parisian lifestyle of old, even though the Eiffel Tower and the beautiful white basilica of the Sacré-Cœur did not yet

---

[158] *An Anglican Adventure – The History of St George's Anglican Church, Paris* – Matthew Harrison, 2005

dominate the Parisian skyline and it is hard to imagine Paris without the familiar tree-lined boulevards of Georges-Eugène Haussmann, but they would not be built in Lewis's lifetime. The beautiful Cathedral of Notre-Dame and the Arc de Triomphe dominated the City of Light.

Paris in Lewis Way's day was on the cusp of industrial and urban growth but agricultural France would be quite reactionary in introducing the new technology of the industrial revolution in England. Paris, like London in 1823 was still horse powered and although philosopher Blaise Pascal is credited with the first Parisian bus service in 1662 it was rather exclusive and the real 'omnibus' was not introduced until much later, in 1828. Clattering carriages and horse drawn cabs on the polished cobblestone streets were still the preferred mode of transport for those who could afford it. Ladies in bright fashionable clothes brushed aside the ubiquitous poor, left behind by the Revolution of 1789. *Plus ça change, plus c'est la même chose!*[159] Paris in 1823 was a city divided between progress, high culture and fashion on the one hand and, on the other, bear and dog-baiting at the Place des Combats. London was not much better, but more expensive.

Having parted company with the London Society Lewis may have felt his ministry to the Jewish people had come to an end and the cause was now in safe hands. This would prove to be true over the decades to come as the Society changed and adapted to become the Church's Ministry Among Jewish People in the 20th century,

---

[159] "The more things change, the more they stay the same", Jean-Baptiste Alphonse Karr (1808-1890)

fulfilling Lewis's dream of reaching out in the love of *Yeshua Ha'Mashiach*, Jesus the Jewish Messiah. CMJ would eventually base itself in the heart of the Jewish State of Israel, in Jerusalem[160], and win the respect of many among the returning diaspora and its leadership.

It should perhaps be noted that in the context of the Hôtel Marbeuf an *hôtel* just means a big house, or maybe a small chateau, it is sometimes referred to as the Château Marbeuf. The Way's new home certainly was a small chateau. The Hôtel Marbeuf had been part of the vast estate of an Englishman called Robert Janssen, a former Royal Navy officer, during the seventeenth century. He had bought up several plots of land until the total area covered over four hectares between the River Seine and the Champs-Élysées, the entire length of the rue George V down to where the Pont de l'Alma crosses the Seine today. It became the Hôtel Marbeuf in 1777 when he sold it to the Marquise de Marbeuf, from whom it was, in turn, confiscated during the Revolution. Sadly, the Marquise was condemned by a revolutionary court, and guillotined. The unfortunate Marquess had evidently encouraged the Prussian army to invade, provided provisions for them and turned some of her land from wheat growing to alfalfa production, thereby depriving the people of food.[161]

By the 1820s this area of land and its buildings were being sold off in lots, but formal permission was required from the French government to open an Anglican church in

---

[160] Christ Church, in the centre of Jerusalem's old city would be consecrated in 1849.

[161] *"Pour avoir sympathisé avec l'ennemi, lui avoir fourni des provisions et avoir semé de la luzerne au lieu de blé sur les Champs-Élysées."*

Paris. Happily Lewis Way had dealt with kings and emperors in the past so he cut out the government, who were trying not to upset the Catholic Church, and arranged for a friendly letter from George IV of England to the French king Louis XVIII. Royal permission was granted on 10th July 1824 subject to reciprocal arrangements for French Catholics in London.[162] All in a day's work for the friend of Alexander I, Tsar of Russia.

Lewis transformed the large gallery or hall adjoining the Hôtel Marbeuf into a chapel and the first services were held on Sunday August 15th, 1824, at 11.30 in the morning and at 3 in the afternoon. The Way family and their staff also lived in the capacious Hôtel and from time to time they would return to England and visit London, Brighton and the estate at Stansted. But in 1826 Lewis Way's executors sold Stansted to Charles Dixon, a wine merchant of London.[163] The family returned to Paris and the Hôtel Marbeuf was their only home. They would stay there until 1830 when Lewis's health, both physical and mental took a turn for the worse.

---

[162] *An Anglican Adventure – The History of St George's Anglican Church, Paris* – Matthew Harrison, 2005
[163] *Enchanted Forest, The Story of Stansted in Sussex*, The Earl of Bessborough with Clive Aslet, 1984, p. 84

Chapter 26

"I am but mad north-north-west. When the wind is southerly, I know a hawk from a handsaw."

William Shakespeare, *Hamlet*

1830 was to be a dramatic year in Paris. Charles X of France and Navarre would abdicate and on 9th August Louis-Philippe would formally accept the disputed crown of France. Revolution was again in the air and on the cobbled streets of the city. In America the revolutionary *Book of Mormon* would be published in Palmyra, New York, dramatically opposing Christian beliefs with its tales of disappearing golden plates, and in England the Duke of Wellington would open the Liverpool & Manchester Railway, heralding a revolutionary new world of steam power that Lewis Way was soon to withdraw from.

In an age of revolution Lewis was not a revolutionary, in an age of reform he was not a reformer. Lewis Way would probably have said he had what is called a 'prophetic ministry' today. He *reminded* people of things that were sure to come, according to the Bible, rather than *predicting* new events and new revelations by way of even newer books such as the *Book of Mormon*. Lewis was always a sound evangelical Christian and, however 'left field' he may have drifted, he remained orthodox and faithful to the Bible, unlike his contemporary Edward Irving.

In late 1829 Lewis's health, which had not been good since his return from Lebanon, began to deteriorate and the family decided he should leave Paris for the winter. It is not clear what Lewis was suffering from but he would eventually be treated by two of the top physicians in Britain, Doctor Henry Jephson[164] and Doctor Amos Middleton,[165] both working at the time in Leamington Spa, Warwickshire. Dr Jephson, according to his obituary in the *Lancet* of 25 May 1878.....

.......*had, until 1848, what was probably the most extraordinary success ever achieved by any physician...... For several years his annual income exceeded £20,000[166], and once reached £24,000.[167]*

Dr Middleton had practiced at the Warneford Hospital in Oxford, then as today a major mental health hospital.

Before the expensive treatment began in Leamington the family moved down to Aix-les-Bains, 350 miles from Paris in the Rhône-Alpes region of south-east France so that Lewis could 'take the waters' and enjoy the bracing fresh air of the Alpine foothills. From there, in a desperate search for relief from his illness they moved over to the hot springs of Bath in Somerset and, finally to the newly fashionable Warwickshire health resort of Leamington Spa in the heart of Shakespeare country.

---

[164] Henry Jephson (1798-1878)
[165] Amos Middleton (1779-1847)
[166] A purchasing power of over a million pounds sterling today.
[167] Journal of Medical Biography 2011

For three years the family struggled, paying heavily for what was often no more than palliative care as his condition grew worse.

Treatment was simple but, apparently, often effective. One of Dr Jephson's methods was to prescribe a diet of "plain meat, stale bread, plain puddings, sherry, black tea and butter – and no fruit or vegetables! Along with regular walks and taking the sulphurous waters at the Royal Pump Rooms this was a better and healthier regime than most people had in Warwickshire at that time and healthier than many today, which may account for some of Jephson's success in spite of the absence of modern drugs and therapy.

Then, on 28th November 1833 the final blow fell…….
Lewis was admitted, by his brother William, supported by the two eminent doctors who were treating him, to the Barford Lunatic Asylum near Leamington.[168]

In spite of the name, Barford Lunatic Asylum bore no resemblance whatsoever to the images of the Bethlehem Hospital in London (Bedlem) illustrated in Hogarth's paintings of *The Rake's Progress* in the 1730s. And even though this all happened nearly two hundred years ago Barford was a progressive and humane institution using the latest psychiatric methods of treatment pioneered in

---

[168] Both Henry Jephsen and Amos Middleton signed the following declaration: *"I the undersigned, hereby certify that I separately visited and personally examined The Rev Lewis Way the person named in the annexed statement and order on the 28th Day of November 1833 and that the said Lewis Way is of unsound mind and a proper Person to be confined."*

France. The private Asylum operated in the quiet village of Barford from 1833 until the early 1850s. It was based in what is now Watchbury House, a large and very attractive 17th century timber-framed building with a gabled porch - Grade II listed since 1983, but no longer a hospital. The large airy rooms and extensive walled gardens speak of a peaceful environment, in spite of the distant hum of the M40 motorway today.

The Barford Asylum was managed by Dr Thomas Morris who had been granted a license to treat up to six residential patients. His wife Ann, who was a Quaker, acted as Matron.

In a newspaper advertisement in 1841 Dr Morris, under the heading, 'Insanity and Imbecility of the Mind', describes himself as:

"Surgeon, Barford, near Warwick, who has been successfully engaged in the treatment of the insane for thirty years."

He says the comforts of home are combined with the "necessary care and restraint" in his asylum. His successor, Mrs Anne Hebert, in 1846, offers "abundant means of out-door exercise, books, music and other amusements, such as daily prayers and the service at the Church of England on the Sabbath." The apartments are described as "commodious and airy." Lewis was well treated in spite of apparently being 'sectioned' in today's terms, i.e. what the Royal College of Psychiatrists calls "being admitted to hospital whether or not you agree to it."

All this along with his detention for seven years and coupled with the fact that he died at the age of sixty-seven of simple "debility" which, though vague, does not suggest any major ongoing condition, just old age for that time. We really must assume that Lewis suffered from mental illness which may well have been treated successfully today with drugs and therapy or even counselling. However, the fact that he was not released like most others suggests more than just a 'mental breakdown' or other time-limited psychiatric disorder. We must also assume he was well treated to have lasted for seven years and it could be that he didn't even want to leave. He could easily be visited by his caring family, and he was.[169]

And we need to make one more assumption concerning Lewis's condition at this time. In his disturbed mind he was probably planning to spend the remains of the family fortune on well-intentioned but possibly unwise schemes. For the sake of the family's future his brother William 'The Bumble' made the decision to have him 'put away', not a very difficult thing to do in those days, for a price. But there is no reason to suspect anything underhanded as neither William 'The Bumble' nor Lewis stood to inherit the family estate at Denham because although elder brother Benjamin would die in 1834 he had a son, also Benjamin, who would inherit and carry on the line into the twentieth century. But Lewis himself had a wife and six children who were not yet married and might be in need of

---

[169] Mary, Drusilla, Anna and Catherine were living at 7 Waterloo Place, Warwick Street, Leamington by the summer of 1841. Mary lived there until her death in 1848.

dowries, or careers. Only the independent Drusilla would never marry.

Lewis would not return to Marbeuf although the property remained in the family. He was eventually replaced as chaplain by Revd Robert Lovett.[170] Whether Lewis wrote or preached during his time at the asylum we cannot tell. He certainly did not publish anything that would find its way to the British Library archives. His last published work, under his pen-name of Basilicus was *Thoughts on the Scriptural Expectations of the Christian Church,* an item reprinted from the *Jewish Expositor and Friend of Israel* and published in 1828 by Hough & Pace of Gloucester.

As our story draws to an end Lewis Way's life moves peacefully towards its close and he looks forward to what he calls "the world to come." What are we to make of his achievements, and failures?

His achievements were, of course, many. He was a father, a husband, a philanthropist, a facilitator and a superb networker. Thousands benefited from knowing him not just as a benefactor but as a friend and a committed Christian. The church in Paris was in itself an impressive achievement which any Christian leader might take a little pride in. St George's Anglican Church is a direct descendant of the Marbeuf chapel though it is now in the rue Auguste Vacquerie, but still close to the Champs-Élysées. The congregation is far more cosmopolitan today, twenty-eight nationalities are represented and only about half its members are of English origin, but Matthew

---

[170] Robert Lovett (1812-1893)

Harrison in his 2005 history of the church says that because Lewis was......

.....the founder, proprietor and first Chaplain of the Marbeuf Chapel, no history would be complete without a short account of his life and his motivations in founding an Anglican chapel in Paris."[171]

History may see him, and in fact does often see him, as an interesting footnote....a slightly dotty Christian philanthropist who gave away a fortune in good works. But looking back over this short biography there is something much more important, much more lasting. In the heady days of Moscow and Aix-la-Chapelle there was a piece of paper, among others, which Lewis presented to some of the most powerful and important men in Europe. It asked a question which won't be answered until the Messianic promises in the Old Testament are relinked in the mind of the Church with their fulfilment in the New. When the Church in all its confused denominationalism turns away from replacement theology, active or passive, and re-joins the Jewish people who founded the Church we might move forward together to that world to come, Palingenesia.[172]

Somewhere between the Jewish Cemetery in Prague and Aix-la-Chapelle Lewis began to understand this break in continuity between the Jewish ancient faith and the Church today. It was not, he realized, for the Church to

---

[171] *An Anglican Adventure – The History of St George's Anglican Church, Paris* – Matthew Harrison, 2005
[172] Matthew 19:28

invite the Jews back in to a church they could not recognise. The Church needed to become recognisable as the one that set out on the Jewish festival of Pentecost, *Shavuot*. Without a true understanding of its Hebraic foundation there can be no true Church, and some might add with Benjamin Disraeli:[173]

"I look upon the Church as the only Jewish institution remaining - I know no other... If it were not for the Church, I don't see why the Jews should be known. The Church was founded by Jews, and has been faithful to its origin. It secures their history, and keeps alive the memory of its public characters, and has diffused its poetry throughout the world. The Jews owe everything to the Church...The history of the Jews is development or it is nothing."

They are, spiritually dependent on each other and cannot afford to drift apart any more. At the heart of his submission to the Congress Lewis posed a question which remains unanswered today but was asked for the first time at Aix-la-Chapelle:

"If in a former epoch the Jews had felt moved by the desire to have a closer look at the claim of Jesus to be their Messiah, would they have been able to recognise the imprint of his character in the conduct of his avowed disciples?...could they have found it in the jails of the Inquisition or in the camps of the Crusade? Could they have hoped for deliverance from these Pharaohs of modern Egypt, these Sennacheribs[174] of a mystical Babylon!"

---

[173] Benjamin Disraeli (1804-1881)

[174] Sennacherib king of Assyria came and invaded Judah (2 Chronicles 3:2)

Could the plenipotentiaries at Aix-la-Chapelle, the representatives of world power at the time fully understand what they were reading after so many centuries of enforced separation? Could they have imagined its extension to the Holocaust and the attempted total destruction of the Church's roots? The Jew Paul said to the gentiles at the very beginning:

.......do not consider yourself to be superior to those other branches. If you do, consider this: You do not support the root, but the root supports you. (Romans 11:18)

This seems to have been, in the higgledy-piggledy way of such organisations, the thinking behind the descendants of the London Society, the Church's Ministry Among Jewish People for the last two hundred years. To reach out in its mission of evangelism, encouragement and education but, above all, to reach out in love, as Lewis had learned in Prague, with the good news of Messiah Jesus, Jesus the Christ.

Lewis died peacefully, surrounded by his family on 23rd January 1840. He is buried at Leamington. The London Society raised a memorial to him at the palatial Palestine Place headquarters. It was later moved to Christ Church Spitalfields in East London. It reads:

SACRED TO THE MEMORY OF
THE REV^D LEWIS WAY A.M.
BORN FEB. 11TH 1772. DIED JAN. 23RD 1840
WHOSE WELL TIMED MUNIFICENCE
PRESERVED THIS HOUSE OF PRAYER
TO THE CHURCH OF ENGLAND AND THE JEWS:
WHOSE UNWEARIED JOURNIES AT HOME AND
ABROAD
LAID THE FOUNDATION FOR MISSIONARY EXERTIONS
AMONG GOD'S ANCIENT PEOPLE:
WHOSE POWERFUL APPEALS
NOT UNSUCCESSFULLY INVOKED THE SOVEREIGNS OF
CHRISTENDOM
TO REDRESS THE WRONGS OF CENTURIES:
WHOSE EXPOSITIONS OF THE WORD OF GOD
AWAKENED THE CHURCH OF CHRIST TO A SENSE OF
HER INTEREST
IN THE CONVERSION AND RESTORATION OF THE JEWS.
THIS TABLET HAS BEEN ERECTED
BY THE PRESIDENT AND MEMBERS OF THE
LONDON SOCIETY FOR PROMOTING CHRISTIANITY
AMONGST THE JEWS,
IN SINCERE GRATITUDE FOR HIS LABOURS
AND IN THE HUMBLE DESIRE TO GLORIFY GOD IN HIM.
"FOR ZION'S SAKE WILL I NOT HOLD MY PEACE." ISAIAH
LXII.I

THE END

Epilogue

The children

Mary Way died at Leamington Spa on 1st June 1848. Drusilla, Anna Mary and Catherine had lived with her at 7 Waterloo Place, Warwick Street in the fashionable 'new town.' They joined in the social life and were often mentioned in the society columns of the *Leamington Spa Courier*. Mary suffered for the last three years of her life from 'softening of the brain' and paralysis.[175] She was nursed by her three daughters and Anna Mary seems to have put off her marriage until July 1848 to care for her. Apart from Drusilla, who pursued her own independent life, the other four surviving daughters of Lewis and Mary married well.

Georgiana Millicent married Henry Daniel Cholmeley (1810-1865), son of Sir Montague Cholmeley, of Woodchester, Gloucestershire. They had two children who lived into the twentieth century. Georgiana died aged thirty-five on 5th May 1855 shortly after giving birth to her daughter Olivia, known as Lily, on 24th April. After Georgiana died Drusilla took care of her two young children, Olivia and Catherine.

Albert had a very successful career as an antiquarian and also rebuilt the Marboeuf Chapel, founded in Paris by his father. He founded the Royal Archaeological Institute and

---

[175] Encephalomalacia

made many valuable contributions to archaeological research. Albert died at Le Trouville, Cannes, France on 22nd March 1874 at the age of sixty-seven. He was married to Emmeline Stanley (1810-1906) with whom he had a daughter, Mary.

Anna Mary Charlotte Eliza married John Ayshford Wise (1810-1870), one time Liberal MP for Stafford at St Mary's Church, Leamington Priors. He had three children from his first marriage. There were no further children. Anna died 15th February 1881 age sixty-seven.

After a fulfilling and sacrificial life Drusilla died at Cheltenham, Gloucestershire on 10th May 1886 aged eighty-one. She tirelessly promoted her father's life and work. Drusilla never married.

Olivia married Charles Edward Kennaway (1800-1875), Vicar of St James' church, Chipping Campden, Gloucestershire in 1845. They had three children, Charles, Agnes and Mariona. Olivia died in Brighton on 8th November 1888 aged seventy-two.

Catherine Louisa married Revd Henry Clarence Pigou (1822-1899) in 1854. They had two children, Mary and Henry. Catherine died 4th May 1906 at Christchurch, Hampshire aged eighty-eight.

Bibliography

Published Works of Lewis Way

1817 Anniversary sermon, preached before the London society for promoting Christianity among the Jews, at Tavistock chapel, Long Acre, May 9, 1817.

1818 *Mémoire sur l'état des Juifs: adresse à S.M. l'Empereur de toutes les Russies.*

1818 A Letter addressed to the right reverend the Lord bishop of St. David's, joint patron of the London Society for promoting Christianity amongst the Jews, by the Rev. Lewis Way, with an appendix [: Letter from an elder of the reformed Jews to the Rev. Lewis Way, Berlin, 1817; Answer of the Rev Lewis Way...; State of the Jews in Poland, the Crimea, etc., Petersburg, 1817; Imperial ukases concerning the Jews, Petersburg, 1817].

1819 Reviewers reviewed; or, observations on article II of the British critic for January 1819, New Series, entitles "On the London Society for converting the Jews."

1819 *Mémoires sur l'état des Israélites, dédiés et présentes à Leurs Majestés Impériales et Royales, réunies au Congrès d'Aix-la-Chapelle.*

1820 A sight of God and a sense of sin: the substance of two sermons preached in Stansted Chapel, on Ash Wednesday, and at St. John's Chapel, Portsea, on Easter-Day.

1821 The latter rain: with observations on the importance of general prayer, for the special outpouring of the Holy Spirit.

1821   The Christian priesthood: a sermon preached at St.
        Paul's, Covent Garden, on the ordination of Benjamin
        Nehemiah Solomon.

1821   Antipas; a solemn appeal to the right reverend the
        archbishops and bishops of the united churches of
        England and Ireland; with reference to several bills,
        passed, or passing through the Imperial Parliament,
        especially that concerning witchcraft and sorcery.

1822   The Flight out of Babylon: a sermon preached before the
        Continental Society, for promoting religious knowledge
        on the continent.

1822   Millenium. A reply to the considerations on this subject,
        contained in the appendix to the Rev. H. Gauntlett's
        exposition of the Revelation.

1823   The household of faith: a sermon, preached to the
        English congregation, assembled at Rome, Sunday, 6th
        April, 1823, for the benefit of the primitive church of the
        Vaudois, or, ancient Albigenses and Waldenses.

1824   *Palingenesia. The World to come,* Martin Bossange, 1924

1827   The convictions and expectation of the patriarch Job: a
        sermon, on the occasion of the decease of H.R.H.
        Frederic Duke of York, preached at the English Chapel,
        Paris, on Sunday, January 21, 1827.

1828   Thoughts on the Scriptural Expectations of the Christian
        Church, by Basilicus, third edition, reprinted from the
        Jewish Expositor and Friend of Israel, Andrew Panton,
        1828

1842   Essays on the coming of the Kingdom of God (by Philo-Basilicus.)
Sermon preached at Tavistock Episcopal Chapel, Broad Court, Long Acre.

Other sources

Anderson, Gerald H. (Editor), BIOGRAPHICAL DICTIONARY OF CHRISTIAN MISSIONS, William B. Eerdmans Publishing Company, 1998

Balen, Malcol, A VERY ENGLISH DECEIT, Fourth Estate 2003

Bessborough with Clive East, ENCHANTED FOREST, THE STORY OF STANSTED IN SUSSEX, Weidenfeld and Nicolson, 1984

Clark, Victoria, ALLIES FOR ARMAGEDDON, Yale University Press, 2007

Dunlop, John, MEMOIR OF GOSPEL TRIUMPHS AMONG THE JEWS DURING THE VICTORIAN ERA, S.W. Partridge & Co, 1894

Ellis, Kirsten, STAR OF THE MORNING, Harper Press, 2008

Gibb, Lorna, LADY HESTER QUEEN OF THE EAST, Faber and Faber, 2005

Grayzel, Solomon, A HISTORY OF THE JEWS, The Jewish Publication Society of America, 1947

Harrison, Matthew, AN ANGLICAN ADVENTURE, St George's Anglican Church, Paris, 2005

Haslip, Joan, LADY HESTER STANHOPE, Penguin Books, 1945 (First published 1934)

Hopkins, Mary Alden, HANAH MORE AND HER CIRCLE, Longmans, 1947

Kohler, Max, JEWISH RIGHTS AT THE CONGRESS OF VIENNA (1814-1815) AND AIX-LA-CHAPELLE (1818), The American Jewish Committee, 1918

Meyer, Louis, EMINENT HEBREW CHRISTIANS OF THE 19TH CENTURY, 1904

O'Rorke, L.E., LIFE AND FRIENDSHIPS OF CATHERINE MARSH, Longmans, Green & Co, 1917

Palmer, Alan, ALEXANDER I, Weidenfeld and Nicolson Ltd, 1974

Stirling, A.M.W. THE WAYS OF YESTERDAY, Thornton Butterworth, 1930

Tattersfield, Nigel, THE FORGOTTEN TRADE, Jonathan Cape, 1991

Wilks, Michael (Editor), STUDIES IN CHURCH HISTORY, SUBSIDIA 10, PROPHECY AND ESCHATOLOGY, Blackwell Publishers, 1994

By the same author

ALL LOVE - A BIOGRAPHY OF RIDLEY HERSCHELL

The true story of a Jewish believer in Messiah Jesus, Ridley Haim Herschell, and of Helen his gentile Scottish wife, who gave up her comfortable life in Edinburgh to share his faith and ministry.

A founder of the modern Messianic Jewish movement and the Evangelical Alliance, this is the dramatic and often moving history of a young rabbi's struggle against his own weakness, overcoming rejection and tragedy as a nonconformist Christian minister. Herschell's journey from 19th century occupied Poland to London's East End and Helen's faith in their ministry is an inspiring story of strength in weakness.

"Well worth reading, highly recommended."
Mary Bartholemew, *The Good Bookstall*

......a gripping and moving account of a relatively brief life lived with courage, conviction, spiritual zeal, integrity and love. It is a delight to read. Henderson has done British evangelicalism an inestimable service by reviving the memory of a forgotten spiritual and intellectual giant.

Mike Moore, *CWI Herald*

For those of us who have been captivated by the Jewish Jesus, and who share a concern for His chosen people, this book has to be mandatory reading.

For further information contact the author on info@htsmedia.com